I0566945

IB ECONOMICS
Internal Assessment

IB ECONOMICS
Internal Assessment

The Definitive Economics [HL/SL] IA Commentary
Guide For the International Baccalaureate [IB] Diploma

Alexander Zouev
Alexandra Laputina

Zouev Elite IB Publishing

Published 2022

Printed by Zouev Elite IB Publishing

ISBN 978-1-9996115-7-6, paperback.

TABLE OF CONTENTS

PART I
THE ECONOMICS PORTFOLIO GUIDE

1. INTRODUCTION

The IB Economics commentary is arguably one of the most interesting, yet most difficult internal assessments you will complete throughout your IB program. The aim of this short textbook is to show you what it takes to write a grade 7 commentary, as well as point out any potential pitfalls and give tips that will maximise your marks. This introductory chapter will review all of the basic information you need to know before starting your commentaries. Thereafter, we will look at where to find good articles, how to use the marking criteria to maximise marks, and also I will present a section on how best to deal with graphs and diagrams.

What is the IB Economics Internal Assessment?

The IA is a vital part of the course and is compulsory for all IB Economics students. It allows students to demonstrate the application of their skills and knowledge and to pursue their personal interests, without the time limitations and other constraints associated with written examinations.

Economics IA is a portfolio of **three** commentaries, each one no more than **800** words. In turn, a commentary is a written work based on a student-chosen article from published news media. Each commentary must link real-life situation from the article with economic theory and a key concept from the IB Economics syllabus.

In other words, your commentaries are aimed to explain current events from the perspective of an economist and demonstrate economic insights into the implications of the article. Each commentary must focus on a different section of the syllabus: Unit 2: *Microeconomics*, Unit 3: *Macroeconomics*, and Unit 4: *The global economy*.

The internal assessment requirements changed significantly for examinations starting May 2022. The most significant change is that a whole criterion is now dedicated to a "key concept." You were likely to have been introduced to IB Economics key concepts in your first year. They are:

- Scarcity

- Choice

- Efficiency

- Equity

- Economic well-being

- Sustainability

- Change

- Interdependence

- Intervention.

I will cover this criterion in detail later in the book. Still, one thing to keep in mind early on is that a different key concept **must** be used in each one of your commentaries.

The new requirements have also increased the word limit for each commentary from 750 words up to 800. The IB Economics Guide clearly states that examiners will not read past 800 words. It may seem like writing this much is difficult, but it is really not. In reality, you will find yourself cutting down the words! Keep in mind that the following are **not** included in the word count:

- Acknowledgments;

- Contents page;

- Diagrams;

- Labels—of **five** words or fewer;

- Headings on diagrams—of **10** words or fewer;

- Tables of statistical data;

- Equations, formulae and calculations;

- References (which, if used, must be in the footnotes/endnotes).

- Citations (which, if used, must be in the body of the commentary);

At the same time, definitions of economic terms and quotations are included in word count and, if used, should be in the body of the commentary. Still, you will see that these are not necessary anymore.

Both SL and HL students are expected to produce **three** commentaries based on separate articles from published news. Under such conditions, same assessment requirements are applied to the IA portfolio at each level. However, the IA weights **30%** of the SL students' final grade, while for the HL students it is **20%**. Nonetheless, both levels should treat their IAs as a safety net that might help them showcase their abilities and potentially be the determining factor in achieving the desired grade.

2. THE ARTICLE

There are several requirements when it comes to choosing the article on which a commentary will be based. Firstly, the article must be published no earlier than **one year** before the writing of the commentary. For example, if you have finished writing your microeconomics commentary (C1) in May 2023, your article must be from May 2022 or later. Secondly, the articles may be from a **newspaper, a journal, or the internet**, but must **not** be from television or radio broadcasts. Thirdly, it is encouraged for students to include articles that are **not too long**, otherwise you will need to highlight the relevant paragraphs. It is also more convenient for the article to be written in the **same language** as commentary. However, if that's not possible, it is your responsibility to provide both the original article and its translated version. Lastly, you must use **different sources** for each commentary. In other words, you cannot pick different articles from the same newspaper.

There are also recommendations on what article to choose for each section of the syllabus. When it comes to the Microeconomics commentary, look for **market failure** articles. With Macroeconomics, the article should clearly focus on a demand-side/supply-side policy and **one** macroeconomic objective. As per Global, focus on a **tariff/quota/subsidy** related to trade, either imposition or the removal of it. Though there are no official topic suggestions from the IBO, it is commentaries on these topics that generally get the highest scores. This is probably because they allow above-average analysis, complex chains of reasoning, and many evaluation options.

Finding a good article is very important, as your further work will be fully based on it. You are likely to take hours to find the right one, though it's better to do that than quickly find a not-sogood article and only later realise that it's not suited for analysis. It can be a headache, but with some patience you will be able to find one that suits you perfectly.

Where to look?

The following sources might have appropriate articles:

- BBC News Online;

- CNN Online;

- Irish Times;

- The Sun;

- Daily Mail;

- The Star;

- Reuters;

- Times of India.

Generally, the article must not be analytical, or your IA will come out as its' summary. Instead, look for a **simple** article that describes an event with **specific numerical data** and considers different **stakeholders**. It is therefore best not to pick economics- or business-oriented magazines (such as *The Economist* or *Financial Times*). Such sources usually do the economic analysis for you, and there is much less scope for evaluation because all of their articles are very well-written and make points that are more difficult to argue against. On the contrary, national newspapers' articles allow you to extract the economic theory and principles from a story. It's also a good idea to note down any potential articles as you proceed throughout the school year. I'm sure that many of you check the daily news or read articles in magazines and newspapers to keep up with current events. Make sure to bookmark any article that you think you could potentially use in a future commentary. In addition, your article should be **forward-looking**. That is, it should look at a policy that is being proposed or has just started being implemented. This is so because articles focusing on consequences of an economic event tend to be analyse and evaluate it by themselves and therefore will deprive you of the opportunity to show your skill.

Guidance

While you should be able to judge for yourself if an article is appropriate, a more effective strategy is finding 3-4 articles and then consulting your Economics teacher with selecting the right one. I'm hopeful that most teachers will be able to give you the green light if you ask for their approval. Understandably, this will vary school to school as teachers are not explicitly obliged to provide approval. However, I'm sure if you ask kindly enough and go see them after class hours they should be able to help.

Analysing the Article

You need to get in a habit of reading economic articles much like you would do in your Paper 1 exams. This means reading them very carefully and noting key words and statements. Once you have picked an article, you will need to analyse it. While your commentary should not include many quotations (otherwise the examiner may view it as an article's summary, rather than your own intellectual work), I suggest you highlight all numerical data in the article that you might potentially apply. In addition, look for links to a key concept. Keep in mind that superficial and far-fetched application of the key concept may lose you up to three marks for Criterion D.

The key to writing a great commentary is finding that perfect balance between introduction, body, evaluation, diagrams and analysis, and concluding remarks. Since 800 words is not much, make every word count and don't waste sentences on things that are just not worth it.

3. STRUCTURE AND FORMAT

Many students feel lost when it comes to starting the commentary. Here is a simple approach to get you going. First, you need to decide on the key concept that fits the article. Keep in mind that you are not allowed to use the same concept in several commentaries. Thereafter, consider the diagram(s) that will reflect the events of the article and sketch them before the writing process. Not only will this step help you to avoid waffling, but it may also draw your attention to the aspects of the article that you have not noticed before. Generally, your commentary will be dealing with the analysis and the diagrams, evaluation, and application of the key concept. You will need to explain **why and how** the events of the article are linked to the theory covered in the syllabus, diagram(s), and the key concept. Avoid the 'scatter gun' approach, where you write about everything you think might be related, and hope to eventually hit the nail on the head. You should choose a few issues which are at the heart of the article and go for a precise and concentrated approach. To do so, plan a rough outline before you dive into structuring you commentary. A good outline should identify:

- the key concept;
- which section of the syllabus the commentary will apply to;
- key terms (commonly highlighted in bold in textbooks for each topic);
- the diagrams;
- core areas of the article to analyse;
- evaluation options;
- the final judgement.

While there is no one way to open the commentary, defining key terms will be a waste of words —definitions are no longer required and do not bring marks. A more effective strategy would be to summarise your analysis in a line or two. There is no need to recap the article, as the examiner has just read it. In the last sentence of the first paragraph, introduce the link between your key concept and the article. The introduction needs to be short and to the point, 5 lines at most.

Place your diagram right after the introduction. If you have two diagrams, put the main one here and the second one before the paragraph that will expand on it. See the following chapter on diagrams for more advice and tips.

Afterwards, analyse the diagram and make sure to link economic theory to the article and information on the diagram. The subsequent paragraphs could be separated by each idea in the article you will be analysing. Furthermore, make sure that you have a meaningful evaluation—it can be either placed within each paragraph or added as a separate paragraph after the analysis. If possible, try to end each paragraph by explaining why the chosen key concept is relevant to what you are saying.

The conclusion in the Economics IA is different to what you may be used to. Because of the limited word count, you should not make a summary sentence or mention the theories that you have analysed and evaluated. You will neither be awarded marks nor penalised for doing so. Instead, the concluding paragraph of your commentary should be a final judgement (you will be able to express your personal opinion here) or a recommendation of a different policy. Surely, you also need to explain the reason behind such a conclusion.

It goes without saying that the font, general format and style should be constant throughout the commentaries. Remember your portfolio will be graded as a whole, so it needs to be consistent. I recommend the standard 1-inch margins. Whether you choose to indent the paragraphs or to use double spacing is up to you, but generally I find the more your commentary looks like a serious piece of academic work, the better. I also don't think you can go wrong with <u>Times New Roman font, size 12, single line space between paragraphs, and full justify</u>. It looks very neat and is my preferred weapon on choice when writing almost any type of paper for university or school. With regards to typography and font emphasis, I suggest using **bold** when you come across a key concept and any related words. Undoubtedly, it improves the readability of your portfolio and makes it easier for the examiner to mark your work.

Details in formatting will signal to the examiner that you are making a deliberate attempt to score highly on the grading criteria. To that end, ensure that each of your commentaries follows this **structure**:

i) Cover page: title of the article, source of the article, date when the article was published, date when the commentary was finished, key concept, syllabus unit, and the word count.

ii) Article: save the article to PDF as it is displayed in the newspaper. To do so, you might use Printfriendly.com. This tool will allow you to delete all the unnecessary information (such as images or advertisement) from the PDF as well.

iii) Body of the commentary, with all diagrams labelled.

After you combine your three commentaries into a portfolio, number all pages and place a bibliography at the very end. There is no need to create an additional cover page for the whole IA. This is the structure that minimises messiness and allows the examiner to easily navigate through the portfolio and find all needed information in no time.

Your teacher might have additional formatting tips. For example, some teachers suggest their students to highlight key concepts with colours. As you will see from the examples provided further in the guide, following such strategy does not hurt. At the same time, it is up to you whether to do it or not.

4. DIAGRAMS

Diagrams are everything when it comes to IB Economics. Whether you are completing a simple homework assignment, answering a past exam question, or busy working on your IA, you can be sure of one thing—diagrams will be needed. In this section, I wish to explain how to best use diagrams in your commentaries, and give advice on how to construct them.

As you will see in the next section, diagrams are of upmost importance in your IA. So much so, that they have their own grading criterion, where you can score up to a maximum of 3 marks. That means diagrams are worth 20% of your portfolio mark. Moreover, this means that you absolutely must have **at least one diagram** in your commentary. However, there is no need to include more than 2 diagrams. Even more, only add the second one, if you are absolutely sure that it is relevant, otherwise you may lose marks for Criterion A: Diagrams. Still, if you have the choice between explaining something in one diagram or splitting it into two, I suggest you go with the latter option.

My first piece of advice as to how to create your diagrams is to **go big**. Don't bother making something small and clustering it with arrows and text. Use the entire width of the page, and make all areas within diagrams clear and visible. Some students have a strong temptation to draw the diagrams by hand; however I don't recommend this for a few reasons. First of all, as I will explain in the next paragraph, creating a diagram digitally is not difficult at all. It will look neat and professional, and you can easily copy and paste the diagram if you plan on re-using it to show any shifts or changes. To say that drawing a diagram by hand will be 'good practice' is not really a legitimate reason. You will get enough practice drawing diagrams by hand when doing past papers. In the IA, the key is to make diagrams accurate and correctly labelled—as if they are coming straight from the textbook.

The best diagrams are ones that borrow **actual facts and figures** from the article. For example, if prices went up from \$1.53/kg to \$1.88/kg, use these as points on your price axis. In addition, consider elasticity when sketching demand/supply curves. Teachers and examiners love this. It really shows that you have read your article and are confident enough to build diagrams that incorporate data directly from the text. It also shows a level of effort that surpasses diagrams that are simply copied and pasted from textbooks/online. Still, do not come up with any data that is not clearly stated in the article. Clearly, your ability to create diagrams with specific data depends fully on the chosen article. Therefore, dedicate as much attention as possible into finding an appropriate source.

Building Diagrams Digitally

While there are many graphing software that you may use to create diagrams, I will recommend using either diagrams.net or MS Word. You don't have to be a particularly tech-savvy person to get to grips with these. Personally, my tool of choice is diagrams.net as it is hosted online (hence does not use much memory space on your PC) and is better suited for graphing purposes. Still, MS Word is absolutely fine in terms of drawing the diagrams. Since it is also more widespread than diagrams.net, I would like to share a few bits of advice to make your life easier.

Let's pretend I have to draw a diagram illustrating the effects of pollution. The first thing I would do is create a **canvas** [Insert → Shapes → New Drawing Canvas]. This is basically going to be your working space. The benefits of having a Canvas are two-fold. First of all it means all of your lines and text boxes will be contained within that canvas and not interfere with the text in the body of the commentary. Any formatting or changes you make will not affect what is contained within the canvas. The second benefit is that if you happen to need a similar diagram to the one you just used, albeit with a small shift or change, then you can simply copy and paste the canvas and that will duplicate all of the shapes and text inside.

Once you have your canvas, adjust the size of it to whatever you like. I strongly recommend filling up at least half the page, and certainly the whole width. Now add a textbox diagram inside and name the diagram whatever you want it to be (for example, Figure 1: *Effects of Pollution*). Make sure the textbox is transparent (no fill) and has no outline [Format → Shape Fill/Shape Outline]. This ensures that your textboxes don't cover up any of the diagram and don't have any ugly borders. For your axis labels I suggest using an even smaller font size.

Make sure that titles do not exceed 10 words and labels do not exceed 5 words—otherwise it will be included in your word count.

To draw the axis of the diagram is very simple. Go Insert → Shapes and choose the straight **arrow.** Now when you are making your axis, hold down **Shift** as you draw—this ensures that you are drawing a straight 0, 45 degree, or 90 degree line. Your main axis will mostly be two lines—a horizontal and a vertical one. As far as the main lines in your diagram (supply, demand, etc.) are concerned, you will use the straight line drawing tool.

One of the most common complaints I hear from students who use MS Word to draw diagrams is to do with the rigid movements of the objects. This problem is easily solved. You must ensure that 'object snapping' is turned off—then you will be able to move lines pixel by pixel as opposed to awkward spaces. To do this, go to Format → Align → Grid Settings and uncheck 'Snap Objects to Grid Lines'. Now just use your keyboards arrow keys to shift things by the slightest amount. Simple!

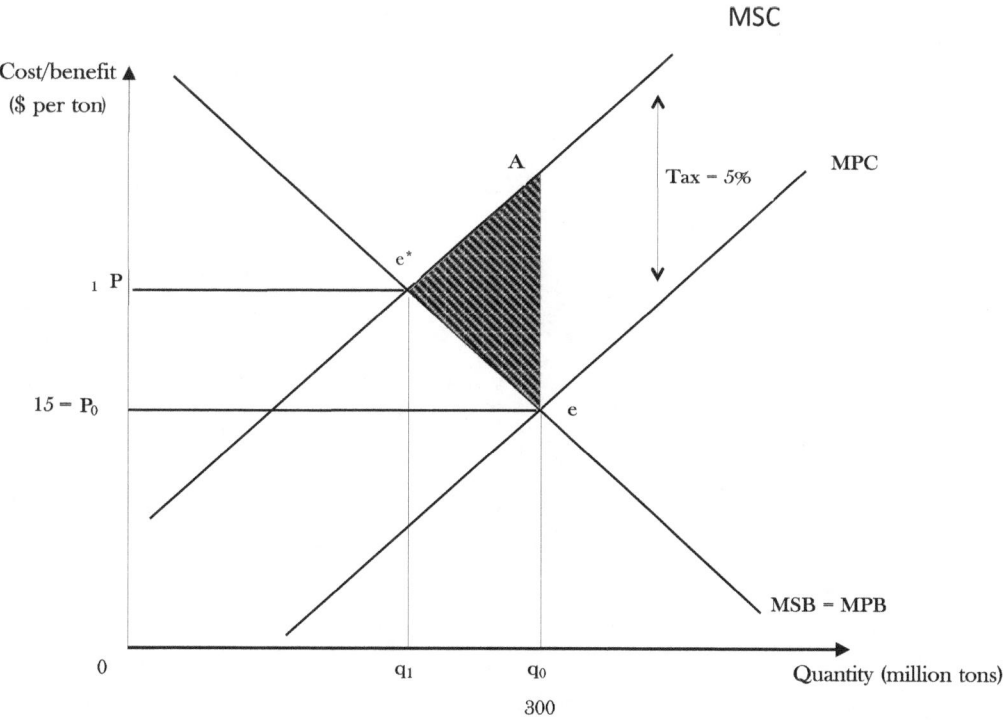

Figure 1: Effects of Pollution

Make an effort to really explore the drawing tools that MS Word has on offer. Whatever your needs, there will be some solution. For example, curved lines (such as LRAS) can be drawn using the curved line tool and then rotated, expanded, and shifted. You can use triangles and boxes to replicate the shading effect found in certain diagrams (such as welfare loss)—just format the shapes shading. In the end you will be able to build diagrams such as the one below in less than 10 minutes.

Explore the other functions and options in MS Word—such as grouping, which will allow your shapes to stay in place even within the canvas. The key is not let your diagrams be limited by anything. Word can make your diagrams look as professional and as pretty as you imagine—you just need to find out the solution. So far in this section I have covered the major slip-ups, but if you discover something that still bothers you, try to Google it and I'm positive that you will find a solution.

5. ASSESSMENT

If you are the lazy type and chose to skip the first few sections of this book, then please read this section with **100% focus**. This is what it all boils down to—everything else is almost irrelevant in comparison. At the end of the day, the only thing that will matter is how well you do on the IB assessment scale. I have reproduced the official assessment criteria that will be used by your teachers and examiners, and we will now go through each section step-by-step to figure out how to score maximum marks along the way.

Similar to external assessment, criteria are set for the internal assessment. Each assessment criterion has level descriptors describing specific levels of achievement together with an appropriate range of marks. Your teacher must judge the work against the criteria using the level descriptors and send his/ her report on the scores to the IB. Then, an examiner will mark your IA and give it the final score.

The first thing to note about the grading of this IA is that individual commentaries are graded one by one, with five criteria and 14 marks per each. Moreover, Criterion F: Rubric Requirements will be applied to the portfolio as a whole. Therefore, the maximum for the portfolio is 45 marks (14 marks x 3 commentaries = 42, plus 3 marks). Such a grading system gives you some safe space to make mistakes: even if your first commentary is not so strong, you may be able to compensate for it with C2 and C3.

Now let's take a look at the criteria in more detail.

CRITERION A: DIAGRAMS

This criterion assesses the extent to which the student is able to construct and explain diagrams.

Level	Descriptor
0	The work does not reach a standard described by the descriptors below.
1	Relevant diagram(s) are included but not explained, or the explanations are incorrect.
2	Relevant, accurate and correctly labelled diagram(s) are included, with a limited explanation.
3	**Relevant, accurate** and **correctly labelled** diagram(s) are included, with a **full** explanation.

In the world of IB Economics, diagrams are everything. A lot of the information in here I will have covered in the section on Diagrams, which should be read first. We are paying specific attention to the grade descriptors. Note the key words used in the top descriptor: *relevant, accurate, and correctly labeled*. In addition, consider the **difference** between the top level descriptor and the one before it—it is only the *full* explanation of the diagram that will help you achieve 3/3.

Let's start with the first one. "*Relevant*" means that you are using the diagrams that reflect the situation in the article. For example, macroeconomic diagrams are irrelevant when it comes to C1. To check for relevance, refer to the syllabus in the official IB Economics guide. You will see that specific diagrams are paired with each topic.

The word "*accurate*" is also straight-forward. You may be using the relevant diagrams, but unless you are shifting your curves the right way, or have curves sloping in the right direction, you could lose marks. Moreover, accuracy means that you have to pay attention to the shapes and sizes of what you're drawing. Does the article discuss how the quantity of a good demanded/ supplied changes with price? Consider elasticity when sketching demand/supply curves. Is welfare loss the central topic of the article? Make sure that you draw a visible welfare loss triangle. Does the article mention a recession? Make sure that you have a deflationary gap in your diagram. "Correctly labeled" should not be overlooked. Examiners pay extra attention to slips in labelling and naming. Not only does it mean that you should label **all curves and axis**, but also **points and areas** that are discussed in your commentary. For example, you can call the welfare loss triangle ABC and even write "ABC—Welfare lost due to underproduction of vaccines" next to your diagram. Furthermore, try to be specific: instead of "D" next to a demand curve, you may use "$D_{before\ tax}$," "D_{2022}," or whatever fits the article. You also need to use data from the article in your diagram (currency, % change/tax, quantity, etc.) Pay attention to the units next to axis, e.g "Quantity, millions of tons" instead of just "Quantity." Still, try not to over-do it: a messy diagram may be difficult to read and explain. Shorthand notation may help you keep the diagram clean. However, only use it if it comes up in the syllabus/textbook or if you've explained it in the commentary. More importantly, "correctly labeled" implies that your diagrams have proper labels! Saying something like Fig. 1 is not enough. Try to be as precise as you can, e.g. "Fig. 1— Change in the Market Equilibrium Price." However, all headings should be of **10 words or fewer** (all extra words will be added to the word count).

The last but not the least important bit of the descriptor demands that diagrams have "a full explanation". This is actually referring to the fact that students often simply throw a diagram in the middle of a paragraph and never justify it. Always make sure you give reasons behind any movements and shifts on the diagram. This does not mean that you have to describe it— such a strategy is likely to cost you both words and marks. Instead, try to answer **why** and **how** your diagram looks the way it does. Examiners hate to see students simply cut and paste a diagram and expect the reader to know what is going on!

CRITERION B: TERMINOLOGY

This criterion assesses the extent to which the student uses appropriate economic terminology.

Level	Descriptor
0	The work does not reach a standard described by the descriptors below.
1	Economic terminology relevant to the article is included in the commentary.
2	Economic terminology **relevant** to the article is used **appropriately throughout** the commentary.

Criterion B is rather straightforward. While there is no need to provide any definitions, you should nonetheless show the examiner that you can confidently use economic terminology. My advice is to create a list of economic terms related to the topics in your commentary and insert them **throughout** your work. You may check the terminology used in your textbook. The general rule is to use all the terms that are in bold/highlighted in your textbook. After you are done with your draft, scan the text once again. Sometimes students use extended descriptions when they can simply refer to terminology instead!

In this criterion, the middle descriptor demands that you simply *include* relevant terminology— something that everybody can do effortlessly. The key is to use the terminology *appropriately*.

This means using it correctly **in context** and ensuring that it is linked with the article.

C: APPLICATION AND ANALYSIS

This criterion assesses the extent to which the student recognises, understands, applies and analyses economic theory in the context of the article.

Level	Descriptor
0	The work does not reach a standard described by the descriptors below.
1	Relevant economic theory is applied to the article with limited analysis.
2	Relevant economic theory is applied to the article throughout the commentary with appropriate economic analysis.
3	Relevant economic **theory** is applied to the article **throughout** the commentary with **effective** economic analysis.

This criterion is a bit ambiguous. It may be hard to understand what *"relevant economic theory"* means. My advise is to link core areas of the article with theory directly from the syllabus. For example, if you've picked an article about implementing monetary policy to battle inflation, open your official IB Economics guide and look what specific aspects of the theory are covered in the correlating topics. In addition, be specific. To continue with the example, consider the correct type of inflation or the specific mechanism of the monetary policy. Of course, do not come up with anything that is unsupported by the article. One more way of ensuring that economic theory is relevant and well-applied is linking it to the diagrams and data from the article. This should be done consistently and not just when the diagrams are introduced. In other words, do not simply copy pure theory from the textbook. Instead, imagine that the theory is a lens through which you are viewing the article.

When it comes to analysis, the general strategy is to convey **why** and **how** the events are taking place. That is, the economic mechanism behind an event and the reason it happened. You may also consider the outcomes of an event. Was there a change in any economic indicators (quantity demanded/supplied, unemployment, inflation, etc.)? Below is a chain of reasoning that may help you grasp this strategy:

(Event) an x% tariff on iron imported to Econland is introduced → (why) without the tariff, Econland imports Q_1 iron as the world price P_w is lower than the domestic price P_d → (how) by imposing a tariff on imported iron, Econland makes it more expensive for foreign producers to export iron → (how) as foreign pass on the tariff burden on Econland consumers, P_w increases to P_{w1} → (how) the quantity of iron imported falls to Q_2, while the quantity of domestically produced iron grows → (outcome) unemployment rate in Econland falls as more people are working to produce iron

This is a simple chain of reasoning, but it clearly showcases the basics of the strategy that I advise using.

You can see that to achieve 3 points for Criterion C, your analysis needs to be **effective** and not just appropriate. This means that you need to do more than simply making reasonable statements. Check if all of your arguments are well-structured and developed. That is, all your ideas are presented in a coherent sequence and arrive at a mini-conclusion. Do not just mention everything you see. On top of that, avoid sentences that sound too generic. Do they look like they can be used for any other article on a similar topic? If so, you're probably being too chatty.

My key advice here is to maintain the **flow** of your writing.

D: KEY CONCEPT

This criterion assesses the extent to which the student recognises, understands and links a key concept to the article.

Level	Descriptor
0	Either the work does not reach a standard described by the descriptors below **or** the key concept identified has already been used in another commentary.
1	A key concept is identified and there has been an attempt to link it to the article.
2	A key concept is identified and the link to the article is partially explained.
3	A key concept is **identified** and the link to the article is **fully** explained.

As I've mentioned in the introductory pages, Criterion D is the biggest update of the assessment requirements. It goes without saying that it is also the most ambiguous one, since both teachers and examiners have little experience with it. Even more, as this criterion is the latest addition, IBO is likely to pay extra attention to your use of the key concept. Understandably, you should also keep the key concepts in mind when looking for the articles and planning your commentaries.

The importance of key concepts is reflected in the marks. You can see that Criterion D: Key Concept is equally important as Criterion E: Evaluation. Even more, if you use the same concept more than once, you can lose up to 9 points. That's 1/5 of the score for the whole portfolio.

Now let's take a look at how to achieve 3/3. It may not be hard to **identify** the key concept. However, its **full** explanation requires a lot of thinking. You also might want to read the official

IB Economics Guide. At pages 12-14, you will find information on the relationships between the key concepts and the course. Stick to these descriptions as the core ideas you should mention when explaining how a chosen key concept links to the article. On top of that, try to present multiple perspectives that showcase this relationship.

Imagine you have picked "interdependence" for C2. One perspective on this key concept would be to show how changes in one macroeconomic objective affect another one, such as the tradeoff between inflation and unemployment. Moreover, interdependence occurs between economic actors, such as the firms and the households. You might also consider how the circular flow of income showcases interdependence. For example, how factor payments from firms to households turn into consumer expenditure. My advice here: get creative! Each of your paragraphs/ supporting ideas should be linked to the key concept.

E: EVALUATION

This criterion assesses the extent to which the student's judgments are supported by reasoned argument.

Level	Descriptor
0	The work does not reach a standard described by the descriptors below
1	Judgments are made that are supported by limited reasoning.
2	Judgments are made that are supported by appropriate reasoning.
3	**Judgments** are made that are supported by **effective** and **balanced** reasoning.

While many students find evaluation hard to approach, there are several clear strategies that allow to achieve the best score. Basically, Criterion E is about evaluating the theory and the assumptions you have chosen to apply with regards to the article.

Let's start by debunking the criterion.

You need to make judgements based on your analysis. In simpler terms, this means stating whether an economic event is "good" or "bad." Try to compare the negative and the positive outcomes of the event from the article and arrive to a reasonable conclusion. Most importantly, back up your opinions. While there are no right or wrong answers here, it is the reasoning behind the judgements that will help you score high.

You might also be wondering when to include evaluation. My advice is to have it throughout your commentary. For example, you may end your chain of reasoning by a small evaluation. However, try to dedicate one paragraph at the end of your commentary to make final judgements. Still, do not waste too much words on Criterion E. After all, it may only give you 3 points.

There are **three** key ways in which you can show evaluative skills:

i)   **Prioritise the Arguments:** instead of just listing points, you could make a concluding statement in which you state which one is more (or less) significant or important and explain why.

Example: *"The least effective way for country X to effectively reduce the negative effects of smoking is to increase taxes. This is because the demand for cigarettes is inelastic and the increase in price due to taxes is likely to result in a proportionally smaller fall in quantity demanded. Considering that <u>in country X</u>, smokers are likely to come from low-income households, they are likely to experience a disproportionally heavy tax burden and have a smaller amount of disposable income left to purchase necessities. This might therefore result in growing inequality."*

ii)   **Long Run vs. Short Run:** it is quite common for the short-run consequences of an economic policy or event to be different from the long-run consequences. If you differentiate between the two (or more! in reality, there is is also medium run) time frames, you are showing evidence of evaluating.

Example: *"In the short run, country X's cost push inflation is a pressing issue. However, if the import prices are growing due to pandemic-related supply chain disruptions, inflation is unlikely to persist in the long run."*

iv) Consider the Stakeholders: a stakeholder is a person or group that has an investment, or interest in something'. Usually, stakeholders refer to domestic producers, consumers, foreign producers high-income people, low-income people, the government, or businesses.

Example: *"A high exchange rate may be good for consumers because it will allow them to purchase imported goods which are otherwise not accessible in country X. On the other hand, it is clearly a disadvantage for those domestic producers who are likely to suffer from the competition with foreign producers. Still, it is likely to push domestic firms to become more efficient."*

My general advice here is to, most importantly, **contextualise** your evaluation using information from the article and what you've already written in **your** analysis. The examiner will be asking whether you can judge an economic theory and an application to a given situation with awareness that the theory may not provide an accurate description. Secondly, make "if"s! You need to question the assumptions of the theory. For example, trade theory of comparative advantage is based on a variety of assumptions that don't actually hold up in real life. Lastly, you can also evaluate your evaluation to arrive at a final judgement.

Useful phrases which you should implement from time to time as evidence of attempted evaluation include:

- ✓ On the other hand,…
- ✓ However, in the short/long run…
- ✓ The most important concern is… because …
- ✓ … is somewhat insignificant compared to …
- ✓ In reality, the theory may not hold true because …
- ✓ This idea is often criticised for …

CRITERION F: RUBRIC REQUIREMENTS

This criterion assesses the extent to which the student meets the three rubric requirements for the complete portfolio.

- Each article is based on a different unit of the syllabus.

- Each article is taken from a different and appropriate source.

- Each article was published no earlier than one year before the writing of the commentary.

Level	Descriptor
0	The work does not reach a standard described by the descriptors b
1	One rubric requirement is met.
2	Two rubric requirements are met.
3	**Three rubric requirements are met.**

This criterion is very straightforward. There is really no excuse for not securing all three points. Note that although this criterion is only applied once to the portfolio as a whole, it is important that you complete the requirements on each individual commentary as you go along. The article requirements are easy to fulfil, as long as you keep them in mind.

THE COVER PAGE

The following information is must be included on each cover page:

- the title of the article;

- the source of the article (including date of access to the site if from the internet);

- the date the article was published;

- the date the commentary was written;

- the word count of the commentary;

- the unit of the syllabus to which the article relates;

- the key concept being used.

On the following page sample cover page that you can use. Remember that you need to make a cover page for each commentary, but no cover page is required for the whole portfolio.

IB Economics IA commentary

Individual cover sheet

Article title	
Article source (including date of access to the site if from the internet)	
Date the article was published	
Date the commentary was written	
Word count	
Unit of the syllabus to which the commentary relates	
Key concept being used	

PART II

SEVEN EXAMPLES OF EXCELLENT ECONOMICS IA PORTFOLIOS

The commentaries featured in this section are all recently submitted IA that scored exceptionally well (band 7) after being moderated by the IBO. The commentaries are presented in the exact same way as they were submitted, without any edits or changes to formatting. We do not retain the copyright of these commentaries, nor is this publication endorsed by the IBO. The Internal Assessments are being re-printed with the permission of the original authors.

1. PORTFOLIO ONE

Author: Alexandra Laputina
Moderated Mark: 45/45
Level: Economics HL

Title of the article: Republic of Ireland to push ahead with alcohol minimum pricing

Source of the article: https://www.bbc.com/news/world-europe-56977667

Date published: 4 May 2021

Date written: 28 November 2021

Key concept: intervention — linked concepts highlighted

Unit: 2 - Microeconomics

Word count: 800

Republic of Ireland to push ahead with alcohol minimum pricing

By Shane Harrison
BBC News Dublin Correspondent

Published
🕐 4 May

The Republic of Ireland's cabinet is expected to push ahead with alcohol minimum unit pricing, despite opposition from retailers.

Retailers fear unless similar measures are introduced in Northern Ireland there will be a surge in cross-border shoppers seeking "cheaper booze".

Health Minister Stephen Donnelly believes minimum pricing for alcohol is a necessary public health measure.

The issue will be discussed when the cabinet meets on Tuesday.

Statistics from the country's Revenue Commissioners indicate that alcohol consumption levels in 2020 were 10.07 litres of pure alcohol per person, only slightly down - 6.6% - on the previous year despite the closure of many pubs and restaurants for large parts of 2020.

Alcohol consumption has remained at about 11 litres per person since 2015.

That is the equivalent of 116 bottles of wine or 445 pints of beer per adult every year.

Getty Images
Scotland introduced minimum unit pricing in 2018 and has seen alcohol consumption levels fall

The proposed measures would see a can of lager costing at least €1.32 (£1.14) and a bottle of chardonnay €7.75 (£6.70) based on 10 cents per gram of alcohol.

The representative body Drink Ireland said it was in favour of tackling excessive alcohol consumption to reduce its misuse, but any measure must be introduced on both sides of the border simultaneously.

Its director Patricia Callan said that unilaterally introducing minimum unit pricing in the Republic of Ireland would "massive pressures on border businesses, and lead toto an increase in illicit alcohol smuggling at the border, all at a vulnerable time for our economy".

But ministers are expected to ignore that advice, citing the Scottish example.

Scotland introduced minimum unit pricing in 2018 and the following year alcohol consumption fell to its lowest level in more than two decades.

Commentary

The article discusses imposition of **price floor** in the alcohol market in Ireland. The government is considering the policy to reduce negative consumption externality from excessive alcohol drinking in the country, on average 11 litres/person yearly since 2015.

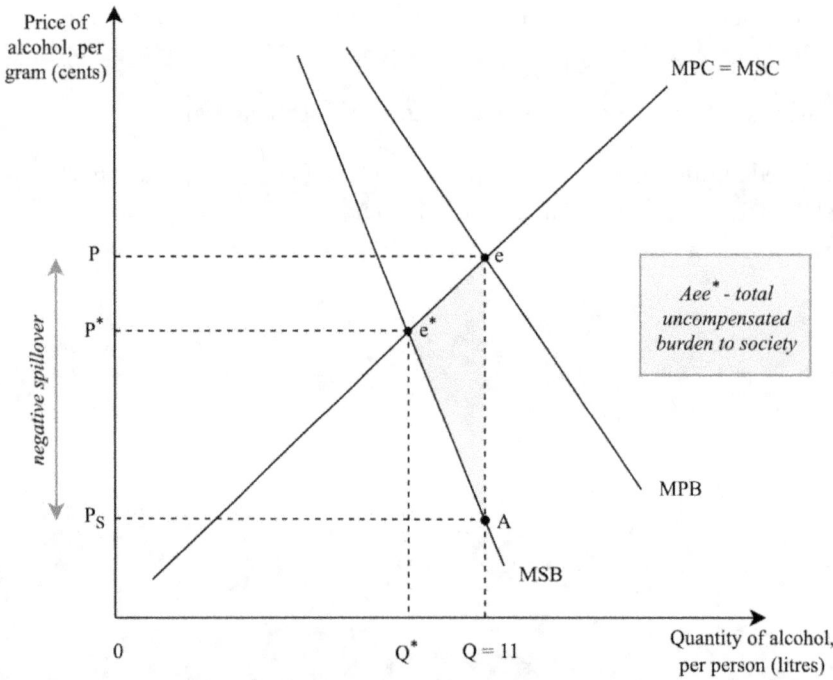

Fig 1. Negative consumption externality in Ireland's market of alcohol

Alcohol misuse causes negative spillover effects onto third parties — pressure on the healthcare system. As marginal external benefit (MEB) is negative, there is a cost from hospitals treating preventable alcohol-relates illnesses, hence increasing ambulance waiting time and using resources to help people with unavoidable sicknesses. As more people use healthcare, more taxpayers' money funds it, and less is spent on other public services. However, rational Irish drinkers do not consider external costs. Despite Covid-related decrease in the alcohol supply and falling consumption, they are expected to return to Q alcohol in medium-term. Therefore, resource **overallocation** to alcohol from society's perspective causes market failure: when people drink above Q*, alcohol consumption private benefits are greater than social (MPB > MSB), and *Aee** welfare is lost. Without **intervention** changing incentives, rational consumers will continue drinking Q alcohol to maximise utility.

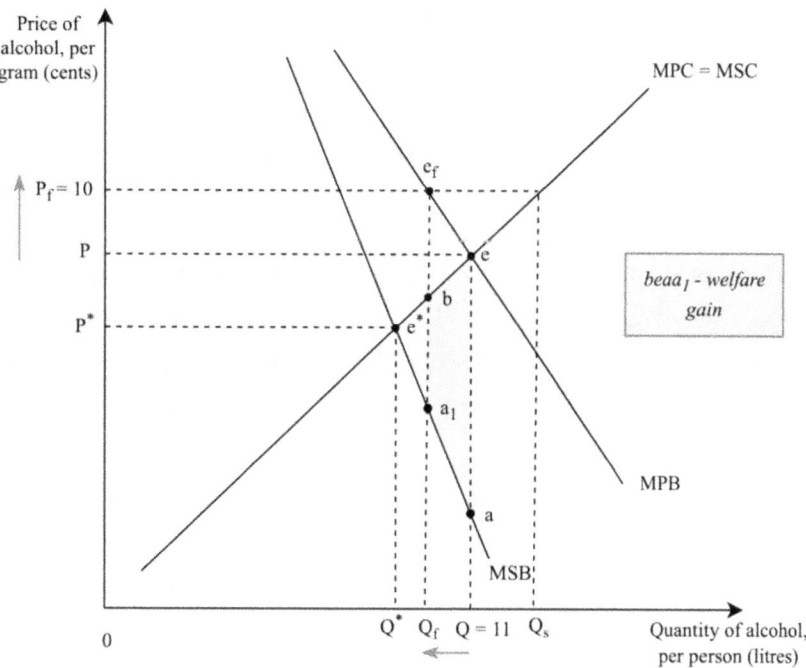

Fig 2. Price floor in the market of alcohol in Ireland

As price floor at 10 cents/gram raises cost to P_f, demand will contract. With Q_f alcohol consumed, external costs will be partially internalized, achieving some allocative efficiency. If lager drinkers are likelier than chardonnay drinkers to overuse alcohol (lager is cheaper), price floor is likely to lead to greater than proportional increase in lager's price, and alcohol abusers will be disincentivised to purchase it. The new welfare loss will be $e*ba_l$, and with $beaa_l$ social benefits will be gained since hospitals will **allocate** more resources to other illnesses. Nonetheless, the policy may not work in Ireland specifically. As lockdowns and supply falling led to only 6.60% decrease in consumption, social drinking is not contributing to alcohol abuse significantly. Instead, consumers' addiction explains inelastic demand. Hence, price floor may not decrease the quantity demanded to Q_f: addicted drinkers will continue consuming at P_f, but causal drinkers will shoulder most of the burden.

Furthermore, price floor is unlikely to reduce $Aee*$ significantly because of smuggling. Assuming **intervention** is unilateral, and the Northern Ireland (NI) alcohol's price does not change, it is more tempting to buy alcohol there. No checkpoints between Ireland and NI make smugglers hard to detect. Hence, Q_fQ_m alcohol could be purchased within a parallel market. As NI and Ireland share borders, alcohol products are going to be close substitutes, and consumers will be able to purchase them for cheaper price in NI. It also depends on the distance to NI: consumers living closer will require less time to cross borders, spending less on fuel. However, people living on south will find smuggling harder, possibly creating low-quality alcohol by themselves and thereby putting even greater pressure on healthcare due to methanol poisonings.

With **increased price** P_f passed onto consumers, legal suppliers near borders will lose customers. This is so because PED is more elastic in alcohol markets near NI's market due to availability of close substitutes. As Ireland alcohol's price will increase to P_f, substitution effect will take place — consumers will be incentivised to switch to cheaper products. In turn, insufficient domestic demand will cause a fall in retailers' revenues who are close to the border, while south retailers' revenues may increase since PED there is likely to be inelastic. If the measure is long-term, alcohol retailers are likely to start making losses and exit the market until a few large firms are left, resulting in little competition and greater market failure. Therefore, negative MEB will worsen, possibly causing more border checking to prevent smuggling. Thus, less government will be spending less on other areas, exemplifying how intervention can lead to even more **intervention** and be cost-ineffective.

Alternatively, Ireland's cabinet may provide information to citizens about alcohol consumption hazards through social marketing. As more consumers will be aware about alcohol abuse's private and social costs, they are likely to decrease consumption. Hence the MPB curve for alcohol in Ireland will shift closer to MSB curve, reducing the allocative inefficiency. While price floor creates excess supply Q_fQ_s, such measure may not increase allocative inefficiency because no surplus takes place. Yet assuming information provision through campaigns are more expensive than **intervention monitoring**, it could be unsustainable for government's budget.

The longer the policy is held, the less people will join the market, while addicted consumers will leave it. As people who are addicted have inelastic PED, generational change is required: **successful** intervention depends on government's **commitment** to make the policy long-term. While the policy discourages using highly alcoholic drinks, so those who don't abuse alcoholic beverages will be less impacted, low-income households may face biggest percentage increase in alcohol price as they are likelier to consume cheaper alcohol. Still, only **coordinated** intervention is effective with porous borders. Considering the unintended allocative inefficiencies arising after price floor, Ireland should implement **additional** measures to reduce them before pushing ahead with minimum pricing. As Smith had a canon of taxation, the government should consider a **canon** of intervention.

Title of the article: New Zealand raises rates to tame inflation

Source of the article:

https://www.thestar.com.my/business/business-news/2021/10/07/new-zealand-raises-rates-to-tame-inflation

Date published: 7 October 2021

Date written: 29 January 2022

Key concept: change — linked concepts highlighted

Unit: 3 - Macroeconomics

Word count: 790

New Zealand raises rates to tame inflation

7 October 2021

The Reserve Bank of New Zealand's (RBNZ) Monetary Policy Committee, led by governor Adrian Orr, lifted the official cash rate by a quarter percentage point to 0.5% yesterday in Wellington, as expected by most economists.

WELLINGTON: New Zealand's central bank raised interest rates for the first time in seven years and signaled further increases will likely be needed to tame inflation.

The Reserve Bank of New Zealand's (RBNZ) Monetary Policy Committee, led by governor Adrian Orr, lifted the official cash rate by a quarter percentage point to 0.5% yesterday in Wellington, as expected by most economists.

Policy makers said they see the economy recovering quickly once a lockdown in largest city Auckland is eased.

"The current Covid-19 restrictions have not materially changed the medium-term outlook for inflation and employment" and "capacity pressures remain evident," the RBNZ said. "The committee noted that further removal of monetary policy stimulus is expected over time."

The move puts New Zealand at the forefront of the exit from ultra-loose policies employed by central banks during the pandemic, with only the Bank of Korea and Norway's Norges Bank among peers to have already raised rates.

The RBNZ's planned tightening cycle could be interrupted by the persistent Delta-strain outbreak in Auckland, which is hurting business confidence and damping the growth outlook.

"Risks around growth are to the downside, but inflation risks are to the upside. That's awkward," said Sharon Zollner, chief New Zealand economist at ANZ Bank in Auckland.

While another rate increase in November looks firmly odds on, "risks are skewed toward something coming along to derail the RBNZ's hiking cycle before its completion," she said.

The RBNZ delivered the hike at an interim rate review rather than with a quarterly Monetary Policy Statement, meaning it won't publish new forecasts or hold a press conference.

The central bank was poised to raise rates in August but held off because New Zealand entered a nationwide lockdown on the day of that decision. Most of the country has since exited lockdown, but the outbreak continues to fester in Auckland, prompting the government to extend restrictions there, and has spread to the neighboring Waikato district.

The RBNZ initiated its last tightening cycle in March 2014, delivering four hikes in quick succession, but needed to unwind them a year later when the inflation it was expecting failed to materialise.

This time around, inflation is already in breach of the bank's 1-3% target band, having accelerated to 3.3% in the second quarter.

The RBNZ said it expects inflation to increase above 4% in the near term before returning toward the 2% midpoint of its band over the medium term.

"In our view, a sluggish pace of global policy normalisation will restrain the RBNZ's ability to raise rates at a fast pace. We see a recovery in labour supply easing skills shortages as borders partially reopen, containing wage rises and muting underlying inflation pressure," said economist James McIntyre.

Prior to the latest coronavirus outbreak, New Zealand's economy was booming. Gross domestic product surged 2.8% in the second quarter, unemployment dropped to 4% and house prices have surged 31% over the past year.

The RBNZ said it is aware that the latest Covid restrictions have badly affected some businesses in Auckland and a range of service industries more broadly, and that there will be longer-term implications for economic activity from the pandemic.

However, the higher vaccination rates rise, "the less virus-related disruption there will be to New Zealand's economic activity over coming years.," it said. — Bloomberg

Commentary

New Zealand (NZ) is at the forefront of **increasing** interest rates from 0.25% to 0.5% to achieve its 1-3% inflation target. However, the **change** of monetary policy will also affect the rate of economic recovery.

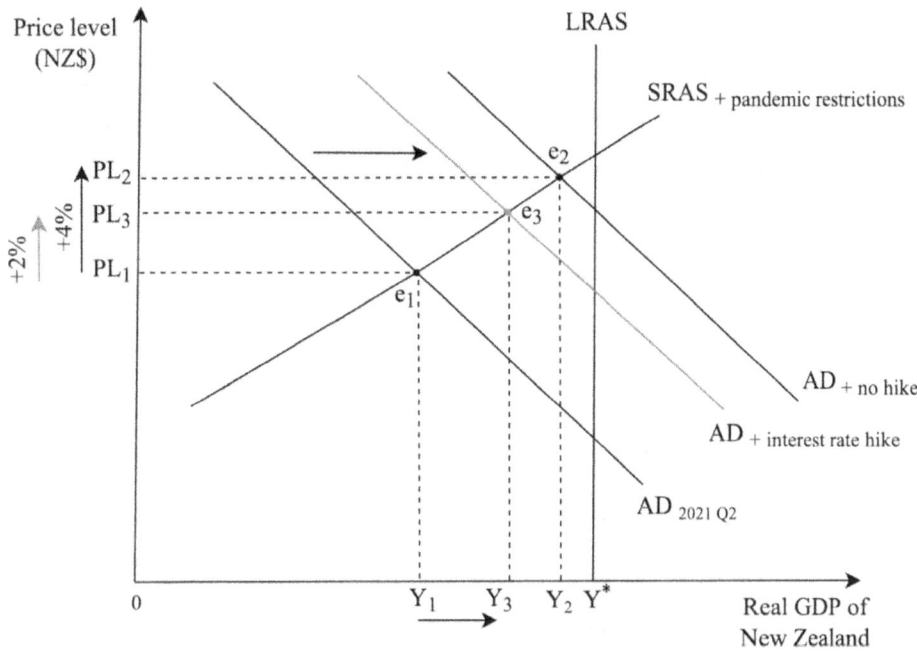

Fig 1. Effects of the interest rates change

As pandemic restrictions have shortened labour supply, thus increasing wages, NZ firms have started to face higher costs of production, leading to 3.3% inflation at PL_1. Yet since most of the country is exiting the nationwide lockdown, business confidence is improving due to expectations of increasing economic activity. If ultra-loose monetary policy remains, investment will return to pre-Covid boom level, shifting $AD_{2021\ Q2}$ to $AD_{+\ no\ hike}$ and causing beyond-target 4% inflation. Changes in the price level are likely to be unsubstantiated since not all businesses, such as those in the service industry, are able to recover from the pandemic quickly. Thus, NZ risks entering a **highly volatile** boom and bust cycle, with a severe recession following the economic upturn. Even more, NZ might enter an inflationary spiral as economic expectations become unanchored due to **frequent** changes in the price level.

As the Reserve Bank of New Zealand (RBNZ) **doubles** the official cash rate to 0.5%, the cost of overnight borrowing to banks increases, hence shifting the supply of loanable funds to the left. In theory, high-street banks pass these costs onto end-consumers of loans, via higher market interest rates. Therefore, firms are less willing and able to borrow money, instead cutting investment financed by borrowing, what shifts AD $_{2021\ Q2}$ to AD $_{+\ interest\ rate\ hike}$ (rather than AD $_{+\ no\ hike}$) and lowers output to Y$_3$. Higher opportunity cost of saving causes withdrawals from the circular flow of income in the form of interest payments and savings, leading to lower money supply and 2% disinflation at PL$_3$. Even more, with borrowing being used by businesses to stay afloat during lockdowns, when weak demand causes revenues to fall, business indebtedness might be high, and 0.5% interest rate might cause some firms to go out of business. Hence, **movement** towards the inflation target conflicts with economic growth, **worsening** the trade-off between the objectives.

The effectiveness of monetary policy will **vary over time**. In the medium term, monetary policy will also lower business confidence. Without forward guidance from RBNZ, firms will find it hard to prepare for **incremental** interest rate changes coming "in a quick succession" as opposed to a single increase. Hence, they will attempt to lower economic activity due to uncertainty of future interest rates, and the recovery will take longer than expected. With already fragile confidence, the policy might further deplete firms' trust in the RBNZ, especially considering that monetary policy tightening in 2014 was ineffective. However, if the rate hikes are spread over time, firms will have more time to adjust their borrowing levels or repay loans completely. In the longer term, the change of RBNZ's focus towards **maintaining price stability** will ensure a stable rate of economic recovery because it will allow businesses to make long-term plans and predictions about future revenues and costs. Furthermore, future recovery of labour supply is likely to assist NZ with returning to target inflation and economic growth.

Even though the change in interest rates is **identical** across NZ, its equitability is not constant. Businesses in Auckland, which are still operating under a lockdown, may find that consumer spending is low. As these firms see borrowing as a necessity needed to cover fixed costs until the end of the lockdown, demand for loanable funds is likely to be inelastic. Hence, Auckland businesses will be disproportionally affected by the interest rate hike, as they will not be able to avoid higher interest payments. Similarly, bigger businesses across country with larger profit margins are more able to take on the debt servicing costs, while smaller businesses without economies of scale are likely to go out of business. Hence, **redistribution** of income will take place, with bigger firms and firms operating in areas with no restrictions experiencing faster growth. Nonetheless, as lockdown is a **temporary** measure, the redistribution is unlikely to persist.

Interest rates are raised **in response to changes** in the external environment, namely unprecedented global pandemic. Hence, monetary policy is implemented to help businesses **adapt** to the post-Covid reality. Moreover, since NZ is one of the first countries to implement tighter monetary policy, its experience will prove useful with determining a global strategy for recovery and for management of similar "**black swan events**" in the future. In that case, successful **inflation targeting** is one of the methods of reducing uncertainty and signalling to the market that economy is under control, thus restoring confidence in the government policy.

Title of the article: China to levy higher tariffs on pork imports in 2022 amid supply glut

Source of the article: https://www.reuters.com/markets/commodities/china-levy-higher-tariffs-pork-imports-2022-amid-supply-glut-2021-12-15/

Date published: 15 December 2021

Date written: 28 February 2022

Key concept: interdependence — linked concepts highlighted

Unit: 4 - Global

Word count: 800

•

China to levy higher tariffs on pork imports in 2022 amid supply glut

Reuters

BEIJING/CHICAGO, Dec 15 (Reuters) - China will raise import tariffs on most pork products next year, the finance ministry said on Wednesday, after the world's top producer rapidly expanded domestic production and reduced its needs for imports.

Tariffs for most favoured nations will return to 12% on Jan. 1, from 8% currently, according to a ministry statement.

China lowered its tariffs on frozen pork in 2020 from 12% to 8% as the country faced soaring domestic meat prices in the aftermath of a devastating outbreak of African swine fever, a pig disease.

Imports surged to a record and remained at high levels through the first half of the year, even as the hog herd recovered and prices fell below production cost by the third quarter. read more

"Adjusting rates in a timely manner can help secure supplies and stabilize prices in the domestic market by reasonably using the international market," said Zhu Zengyong, researcher with the Chinese Academy of Agricultural Sciences.

The higher rates will further slow imports from top exporters like the United States and Spain that have already dropped sharply in recent months.

Most U.S. pork shipments to China face a 25% retaliatory tariff imposed during the trade war between Washington and Beijing, in addition to the most favoured nations (MFN) tariff.

"After years of working to remove tariffs, we are disappointed to see China's foreign ministry announce the increase in MFN tariffs on pork," said Maria Zieba, assistant vice president of international affairs for the National Pork Producers Council in Washington.

"This is especially concerning given ongoing issues with African swine fever and the high demand for pork in China."

October pork arrivals in China fell by 40% on the prior year to 200,000 tonnes, though imports in the year to date have only slipped 8% on a year ago to 3.34 million tonnes, according to customs data.

"Any increase in tax makes it more challenging to exporters," said Joel Haggard, senior vice president for the Asia Pacific at the U.S. Meat Export Federation.

Reporting by Hallie Gu and Dominique Patton in Beijing and Tom Polansek in Chicago; Editing by Mark Potter and Cynthia Osterman

Commentary

The article discusses China reinstating tariffs on pork for most favoured nations (MFN) from 8% to 12% after a period of domestic supply-side shock in the industry and levying a 25% retaliatory tariff on the USA. Thus, **linked market outcomes** of Chinese producers (CP) and MFN producers will change.

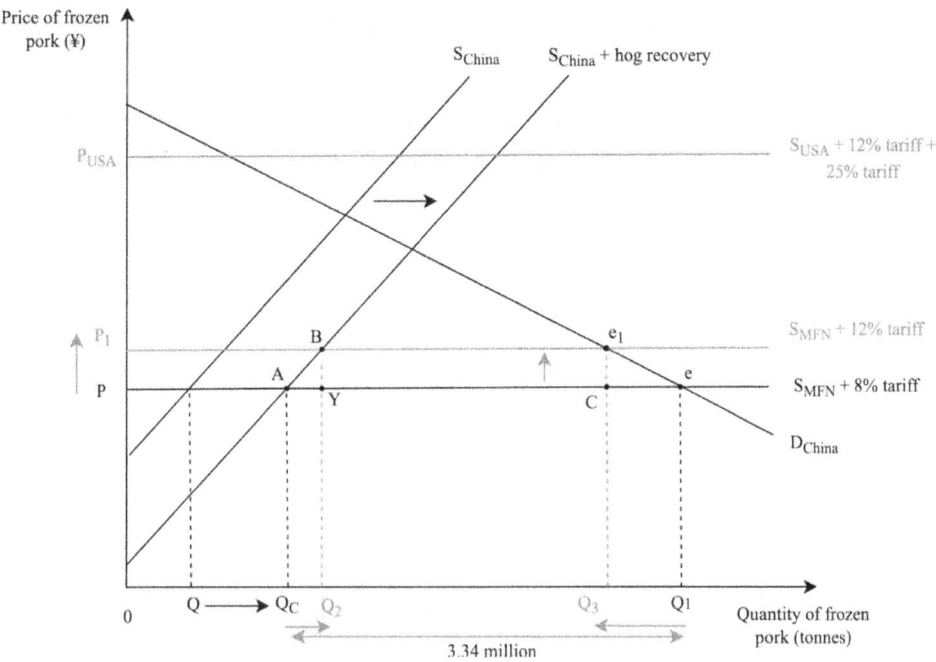

Fig 1. Hog recovery and tariffs on pork imports

Chinese and MFN pork firms are **interdependent** in terms of revenues and market shares because they are competing for D_{China} which is assumed to be fixed in the short run. At e, with 8% tariffs and a pig disease outbreak, China was importing QQ_1 frozen pork, while Q pork was produced domestically. While foreign producers occupied majority of the market and earned QQ_1eX revenue, CP were only earning $PXQ0$ revenue. With the recovery of the hog herd in the beginning of 2021, less medicine was required to sustain pigs. Falling costs of factors of production thus shifted domestic supply S_{China} to S_{China1}, increasing output to Q_C. Therefore, CP started earning XAQ_CQ more revenue, which was lost by MFN producers, meaning that improvement in market outcomes for CP happened **at the expense** of MFN.

51

CP also lowered pork prices below their costs of production to attract more domestic consumers. Even so, they remained outcompeted by MFN imports, what suggests that MFN producers have a **comparative advantage** in pork production and can produce it with lower **opportunity costs.** Hence, by imposing a higher tariff, China may be able to compensate for domestic producers' inefficiency. However, if the inefficiency arises from a temporary pig disease outbreak, increasing tariffs may be excessive: after supply recovery has started to take place, already in October 2021 imports were 40% smaller than in the previous year.

The increase to 12% tariff will also increase the costs of supplying to China, assuming that the tariff is paid by importers. MFN producers are likely to pass higher costs onto consumers by increasing the price of pork to P_1. Seeing that the reduction of the tariff in 2020 caused imports to surge, MFN pork is likely to have elastic PED due to the ease of switching between substitutes — other types of meat as well as domestically produced pork. Therefore, the quantity of imports is likely to fall significantly, to Q_2Q_3, with MFN producers facing majority of the tariff **burden.** In turn, export revenue for MFN producers will also fall to $Q_2Q_3e_1B$.

CP will partly occupy MFN's market share and increase output to Q_2. Higher producer surplus P_1PP_A will indicate that Chinese pork industry is becoming more **protected**, and CP are earning more revenues. However, if CP do not recover from the supply shock and less than Q_2 pork is available when the tariffs are raised, a shortage in the market of pork will take place, indicating that CP are not able to meet the needs of the domestic market. Even more, since pork will become less affordable at P_1, CP's increased producer surplus will also lead to **worsening** of the consumer surplus. If CP achieve greater efficiencies due to economies of scale, prices may fall again. Nonetheless, this is unlikely to take place in the near-term due to time lags in pork production.

As US producers will face an additional 25% tariff, P_{USA} will be even higher than P_1. Assuming that pork is homogenous and Q_3 pork can be supplied by China and MFN at P_1, no rational Chinese consumer will buy USA pork for P_{USA}. Hence, US imports to China will be reduced to 0, ceteris paribus. This will lead to a surplus in China's current account with the USA. Thus, yuan is likely to **appreciate against** the US dollar, making it more expensive for USA to import from China and thus potentially worsening the **trade relationship** between the two countries. Nonetheless, if pork trade constitutes only a small percentage of trade in goods between the two countries, it is unlikely to affect exchange rates.

Lowered interdependence will result in global inefficiency. This is so because greater trade barriers were likely to be announced unexpectedly. Considering that most large companies implement long-term planning strategies, they may not have time to adjust their production quantities. The welfare loss Cee_1 thus represents pork that was produced by MFN to export, but never bought by China. Furthermore, ABY welfare will still be lost as production in China is more inefficient. Still, as Chinese pork industry becomes more independent, the inefficiency may be solved in the medium-term. Moreover, since MFN may still export Q_3Q_1 pork to other countries, it is likely that they will become more integrated with new importers.

Bibliography

1.	Hoang, P., Wray, S. and Chakraborty, T., 2020. *Economics for the IB Diploma*. London: Hodder Education Group.

2.	Tragakes, E., 2012. *Economics for the IB Diploma*. 2nd ed. Cambridge: Cambridge University Press.

2. PORTFOLIO TWO

Author: Ella Kang
Moderated Mark: 41/45
Level: Economics SL

Commentary 1

Unit of the syllabus	Microeconomics
Title of the article	"Indiana lawmakers discuss 1st cigarette tax hike since 2007"
Source of the article	https://www.chicagotribune.com/suburbs/post-tribune/ct-ptb-indiana-cigarette-tax-st-0202-20210201-dr7doufqsbeu7ivzxzm7k6iala-story.html
Date the article was published	1 February 2021
Date the article was accessed	17 October 2021
Date the commentary was written	22 October 2021
Key concept	Intervention
Word count	800

POST-TRIBUNE SUBURBS

Indiana lawmakers discuss 1st cigarette tax hike since 2007

By **TOM DAVIES**
POST-TRIBUNE | FEB 01, 2021

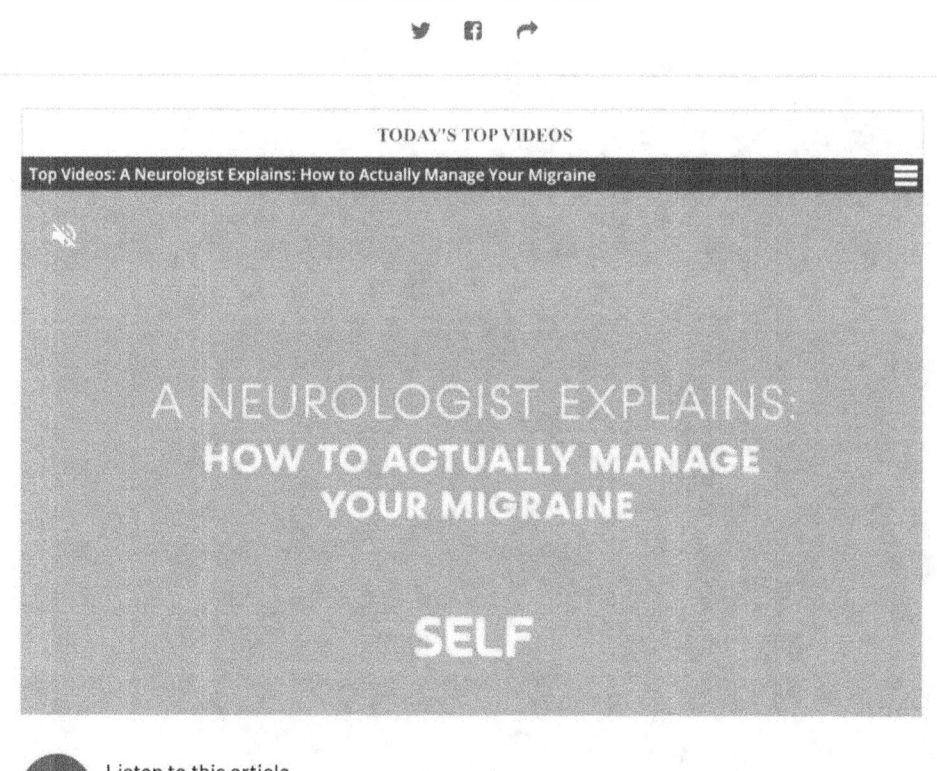

TODAY'S TOP VIDEOS

Top Videos: A Neurologist Explains: How to Actually Manage Your Migraine

A NEUROLOGIST EXPLAINS:
HOW TO ACTUALLY MANAGE
YOUR MIGRAINE

SELF

Listen to this article

Indiana could increase its cigarette tax for the first time in more than a decade and impose a new state tax on vaping liquids under a proposal taken up Monday by state lawmakers.

The proposal would add $1 to the state's current 99.5 cents per pack cigarette tax and has the backing of many health organizations and business groups as a way to discourage smoking and reduce Indiana's high smoking rate.

It also would charge a 39% tax on the liquids used in e-cigarettes, which bill sponsor Republican Rep. Julie Olthoff, of Crown Point, said would be roughly equivalent to the cigarette tax.

Julie Olthoff - Original Credit: Post-Tribune (Provided by Julie Olthoff / HANDOUT)

Bryan Hannon, an American Cancer Society lobbyist, told the Indiana House Public Health Committee that increasing the cost for vaping was needed so that it didn't become more appealing to cigarette smokers.

"The importance of tobacco tax parity in public health is to make sure when you raise the price on one tobacco product, you're raising the price on other tobacco products so as not to encourage switching," Hannon said.

[Most read] One dead, one critically injured in chemical explosion at production plant in Hampshire »

Some supporters want an even greater increase of $2 per pack in the cigarette tax.

Indiana Chamber of Commerce President Kevin Brinegar argued the state's high smoking rates increased health care costs for businesses and hurt Indiana's economic competitiveness.

Indiana's 21.1% smoking rate among adults was the 4th highest in the country for 2018, according to the federal Centers for Disease Control and Prevention. Nationwide tracking by the Campaign for Tobacco-Free Kids lists Indiana's current cigarette tax as the country's 39th highest, falling below all neighboring states.

The Indiana House last backed a $1 per pack increase in 2017, only to see the move fail as the state Senate as Republican Gov. Eric Holcomb also opposed it. Previous attempts to implement a vaping products tax have also failed in the Republican-dominated Legislature.

Donald Rainwater, who was the Libertarian candidate for governor last year, urged lawmakers to consider the "adverse economic outcomes" for business that have struggled during the COVID-19 pandemic if the tax hike was to cut their sales of cigarettes and vaping products.

No one from the Holcomb administration spoke during Monday's committee hearing, but the governor's top health adviser said during the state health department's budget hearing last week that lawmakers should make any cigarette tax increase large enough to be "worthwhile" and noted Indiana's status with the region's lowest tax.

Indiana saw a 20% decrease in the consumption of cigarettes following its 2007 tax increase of 44 cents per pack, state Health Commissioner Dr. Kristina Box said.

"Most importantly, what we saw was a decrease in new starts in our most vulnerable population, like our pregnant patients," Box said.

Some Democrats on the House health committee questioned why more of the nearly $290 million in estimated revenue from the cigarette and vaping taxes wasn't being directed to health programs. A legislative report projected that more than 60% of the money would go to the state's general fund and pension programs, with much of the remainder split between several health programs.

Republican Rep. Brad Barrett of Richmond, the health committee chairman, said he agreed the committee should weigh in on possible uses for the tax revenue and that he expected it would consider amendments to the proposal next week.

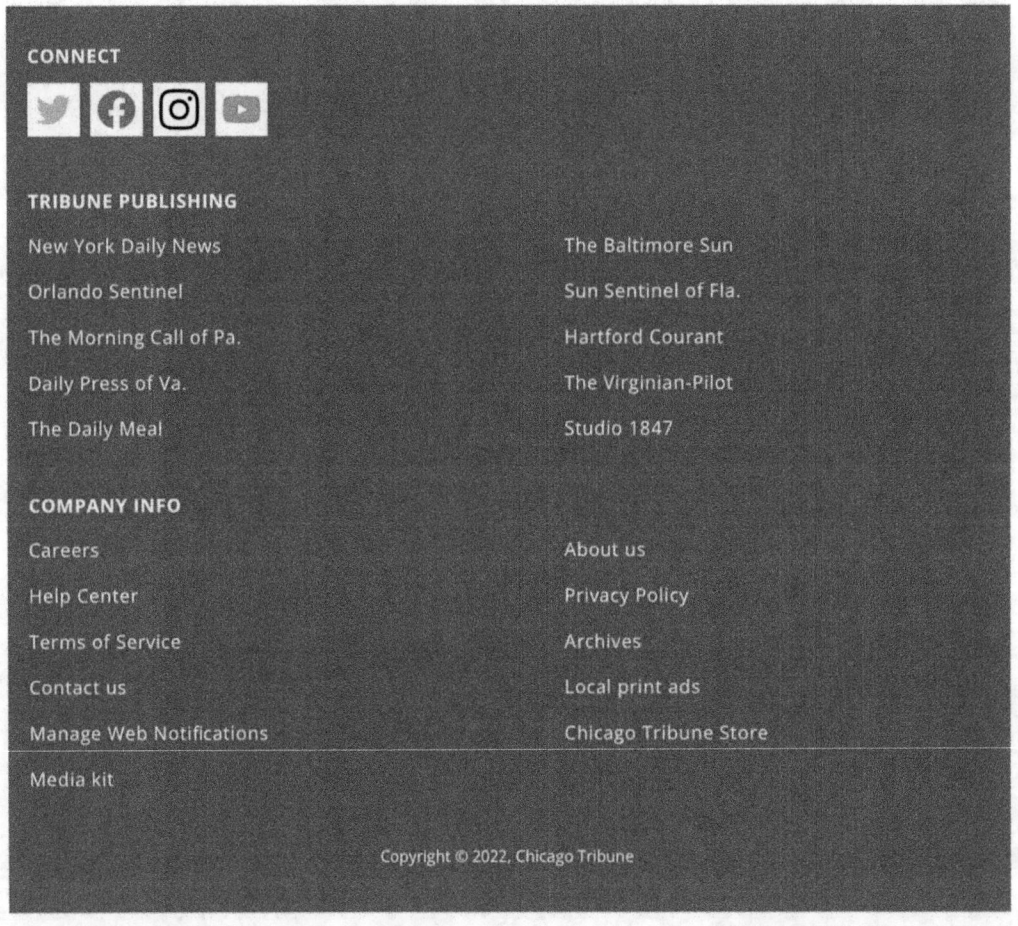

Commentary

This article discusses Indiana's proposal to increase tax on cigarettes by US$1 on the existing 99.5 cents/pack, and by 39% on vaping liquids to "discourage smoking and reduce Indiana's high smoking rate". Cigarettes are demerit goods; consumption of such socially undesirable goods negatively impacts consumers and generates negative externalities for third parties. In Indiana, high smoking rates and related health problems "increased health care costs for businesses and hurt Indiana's economic competitiveness".

The key concept of this commentary is intervention. To resolve the problems, Indiana's government intervened with indirect excise tax, a specific tax on cigarettes that manufacturers pay and in turn increases the cost at purchase for consumers.

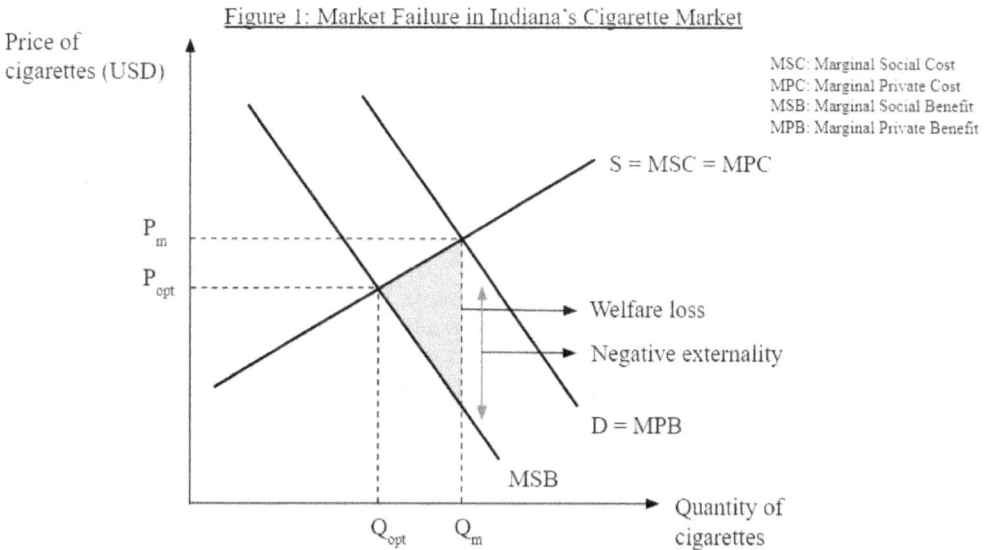

Figure 1: Market Failure in Indiana's Cigarette Market

Market equilibrium is at (Q_m, P_m) where demand or MPB intersects with supply or MPC. While individuals continue the cigarette overconsumption to maximize their benefits, third parties suffer from additional costs, the negative externalities. Thus, private benefits are greater than social benefits and MPB is over MSB. Social optimum is then obtained at (Q_{opt}, P_{opt}) where MSB intersects with MSC. The shaded region between Q_m and Q_{opt} is overallocation of cigarettes compared to its production, thus welfare loss for society.

61

Although free markets are efficient in organizing economic activities, Indiana's cigarette market failed to achieve allocative efficiency, indicating market failure. This is sufficient reason for government intervention, indirect tax being imposed as solution.

Figure 2: Effect of Indirect Tax in Indiana's Cigarette Market

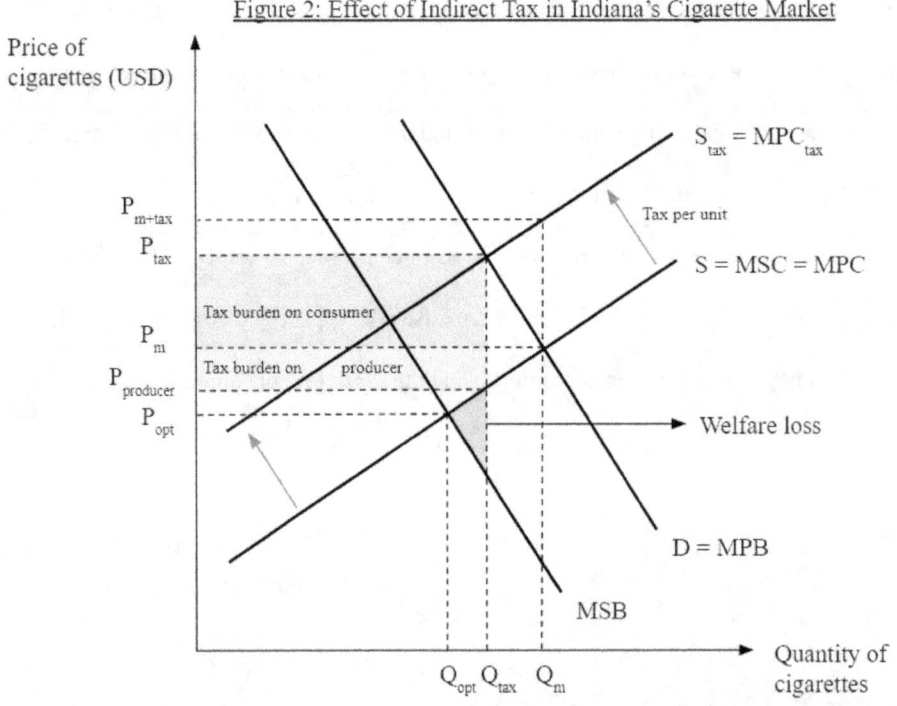

Figure 2 depicts the effects of intervention as indirect tax in Indiana's cigarette market. With higher costs of production for producers, less is produced at Q_{tax}. Therefore, reduced quantity is presented as the leftward shift of S = MPC to S_{tax} = MPC_{tax} while MSC remains as social costs did not increase. To recover the additional production costs, producers increase the price of cigarettes for consumers from P_m to P_{m+tax}. Consequently, higher price leads to a fall in demand for cigarettes at all prices. Because cigarettes are oversupplied at P_{m+tax}, producers then lower the price to P_{tax}, changing market equilibrium from (Q_m, P_m) to (Q_{tax}, P_{tax}) with decreased welfare loss. Producers are now worse off with revenue reduced from (Q_m, P_m) to (Q_{tax}, $P_{producer}$). Moreover, addictive cigarettes are price inelastic, meaning price change causes relatively small changes in demand. Consumers' tax burden of

$(P_{tax} - P_m, Q_{tax})$ is therefore more affected than producers' tax burden of $(P_m - P_{producer}, Q_{tax})$ since producers can supply cigarettes at a higher price $(P_{tax} > P_m)$ to pass on the burden to consumers. Hence, with tax, consumers suffer from purchasing less at this increased price.

Moreover, cigarette businesses "that have struggled during the COVID-19 pandemic" are disadvantaged by the "adverse economic outcomes" of tax. In addition to previously decreased sales, tax further reduces the quantity demanded and thus, the firms' profits. If losses are prevalent in the long-term, manufacturers may decrease or cease their production, reducing the size of domestic industry and causing unemployment in society.

In 2018, Indiana had adult smoking rates of 21.1%, the fourth-highest nationwide. Since such a large proportion is dependent on price inelastic cigarettes, consumption does not change drastically in a short period of time, meaning negative externalities of consumption might not be eliminated completely. Likewise, all individuals are to pay higher fixed prices, arousing income inequality by affecting low to middle-income households. The regulation also may not be effective for higher-income households as they continue the consumption with their disposable income for their own benefits.

Furthermore, because of the price inelastic nature of cigarettes, indirect tax is less effective in the short run. If consumers have time to change consumption habits and find alternatives for cigarettes, a greater reduction in smoking rates is expected. Yet, Indiana's policy seems to be successful in its aim to lessen the overall consumption since a substitute, e-cigarettes, are also being taxed "as roughly equivalent to the cigarettes" so that they "[don't] become more appealing to cigarette smokers".

Following its tax increase in 2007, Indiana's most vulnerable population like pregnant patients decreased their cigarettes consumption. Similarly, if smokers consume fewer cigarettes after the new regulation, the whole society's health would improve in the long run, reducing negative externalities and achieving the government's aim.

Indirect tax also allows high government revenue of "nearly $290 million", 60%

of which will be allocated to fund merit goods, especially "to the state's general fund and

pension programs [and] several health programs". This expenditure will promote the

extended well-being of the population.

Overall, intervention in the form of indirect tax on cigarettes is beneficial to

society in the long-term as it corrects market failure and improves society's health.

Alternatively, to minimize the concerns of time lag, income inequality, and unemployment,

Indiana's government could intervene with supply-side policies like educating population

about the negative impacts of smoking. Raising public awareness will then reduce

consumption and welfare loss, but high government expenditure and opportunity costs might

be involved.

Unit of the syllabus	Macroeconomics
Title of the article	"Budget 2021: S$11 billion Covid-19 Resilience Package to fund immediate public health measures, still-ailing sectors"
Source of the article	https://www.todayonline.com/singapore/budget-2021-s11-billion-covid-19-resilience-package-fund-immediate-public-health-measures
Date the article was published	16 February 2021
Date the article was accessed	19 December 2021
Date the commentary was written	27 December 2021
Key concept	Economic well-being
Word count	800

Budget 2021: S$11 billion Covid-19 Resilience Package to fund immediate public health measures, still-ailing sectors

Some government support measures such as the Jobs Support Scheme will continue for some sectors, but other schemes to keep the economy afloat will cease.

BY JANICE LIM

Published February 16, 2021
Updated February 17, 2021

- **An S\$11 billion package will fund Singapore's vaccination programme and the maintenance of existing public health measures**
- **It will also go towards supporting the tourism, aerospace aviation, arts and culture and sports sectors**
- **DPM Heng announced that he will allocate another S\$5.4 billion to the SGUnited Jobs and Skills Package**
- **Several government support schemes launched in 2020 will be allowed to expire**

SINGAPORE — A new S\$11 billion Covid-19 Resilience Package has been launched to address Singapore's immediate needs to safeguard public health and to provide targeted support to workers and sectors that are still under stress. At the same time, some of the relief schemes unveiled last year will be allowed to lapse.

Deputy Prime Minister Heng Swee Keat announced this new package in his Budget speech on Tuesday (Feb 16).

He noted that the Singapore economy is projected to grow between 4 per cent and 6 per cent this year, but this will be unevenly distributed. This is because some parts of the economy will continue to be battered by the Covid-19 crisis.

SAFEGUARDING PUBLIC HEALTH

READ ALSO
Budget 2021: Key announcements and highlights

To continue efforts in curbing the spread of the coronavirus, Mr Heng, who is also Finance Minister, said that S\$4.8 billion of the package will be dedicated towards public health and safe-reopening measures.

These include expanding the nation-wide vaccination programme and maintaining existing precautionary measures, contact tracing system, testing regime and safe-distancing requirements.

"Vaccinating our people is key. We started our vaccination programme late last year. As at Feb 14 this year, close to 250,000 people have received their first dose of the Covid-19 vaccine, of which 55,000 have also received their second dose," Mr Heng said.

"I strongly urge Singaporeans and residents who are medically eligible to take the vaccine when your turn comes."

SUPPORT FOR WORKERS AND BUSINESSES

1. Extension of the Job Support Scheme

READ ALSO

More than 140,000 employers to receive S$5.5 billion in Jobs Support Scheme payouts from Oct 29

The Job Support Scheme — under which companies received subsidies for at least 10 per cent of the wages they paid out for most of 2020 — will be extended, but only for sectors that are still affected by the economic disruption brought about by the global pandemic.

Companies in the aerospace, aviation and tourism sectors will continue to receive wage support until September this year, a six-month extension from the original March 31 expiry date.

The Government will subsidise 30 per cent of wages that the companies in these sectors will have to pay their workers between April and June this year. The subsidy will be given out in September.

From July to September this year, there will be a 10 per cent support for wages, which will be disbursed in December.

These companies are now receiving 50 per cent in wage subsidies.

The scheme will also be extended by three months for firms in the retail, food services, built environment and arts and culture sectors. They are now receiving 30 per cent subsidies until March this year.

READ ALSO

DPM Heng stresses need to forge partnerships, continue prudent spending in Emerging Stronger Together Budget 2021

For wages to be credited between April and June this year, these firms will receive 10 per cent subsidies, which will be paid out in September.

This scheme will stop there after for firms in these sectors.

For all other sectors still receiving help, support will not be extended after March 31 under the scheme.

Mr Heng said the extension for the selected sectors will cost S$700 million. The Government has committed more than S$25 billion in wage subsidies, which has helped more than 155,000 employers for up to 17 months so far.

2. SGUnited Jobs and Skills Package

Mr Heng also said that he will allocate another S$5.4 billion to the SGUnited Jobs and Skills Package. This is on top of the S$3 billion channelled to a whole range of schemes that seek to create jobs and traineeships opportunities for Singaporeans last year.

READ ALSO
250,000 in Singapore have received first dose of Covid-19 vaccine: PM Lee

Out of the S$5.4 billion, S$5.2 billion will be set aside for the Jobs Growth Incentive, which has been extended by seven months to September 2021.

The scheme provides companies with up to one year of salary support from the Government from the month that each new Singapore worker was hired since September last year.

Older workers, those with disabilities and ex-offenders will be given 1.5 years of salary support.

Other programmes for fresh graduates and mid-career workers under the SGUnited series, where the Government provides training allowance, will also be extended for one more year until March 31, 2022.

Mr Heng said that the next phase of the SGUnited Jobs and Skills Package aims to create 200,000 jobs, 35,000 traineeships and training opportunities this year.

Since its launch in May until the end of last year, nearly 76,000 people were placed in jobs, traineeships, attachments and skills training, he added.

SUPPORT FOR HARD-HIT SECTORS

With global travel unlikely to recover as international borders remain close, Mr Heng said that the Government will provide S$870 million to support the aviation sector from this year's Budget.

At the end of last month, total passenger movements at Changi Airport were only about 2 per cent of what they were pre-Covid-19.

"I expect the aviation sector to use this lull to sustain and upgrade its capabilities and to prepare for the recovery," he said.

In a media statement, Singapore Airlines' chief executive officer Goh Choon Phong said that the Budget measures will help the company's plans to navigate the disruptions caused by the Covid-19 pandemic, yet remain nimble and flexible enough to seize opportunities that may come when international borders open.

"The foundations that we build during this crisis will put us in a strong position to overcome the current challenges and cement our leading position in a fast-changing aviation environment," Mr Goh said.

To help the arts and culture and sports sectors, Mr Heng said that the Government will set aside S$45 million to help support businesses and self-employed individuals in these sectors.

Last year, the Ministry of Culture, Community and Youth rolled out a S$55 million Arts and Culture Resilience Package and a S$50 million Sports Resilience Package.

For the land transport sector, S$133 million will be allocated to the Covid-19 Driver Relief Fund, which replaced the Special Relief Fund for taxi and private-hire car drivers from January this year.

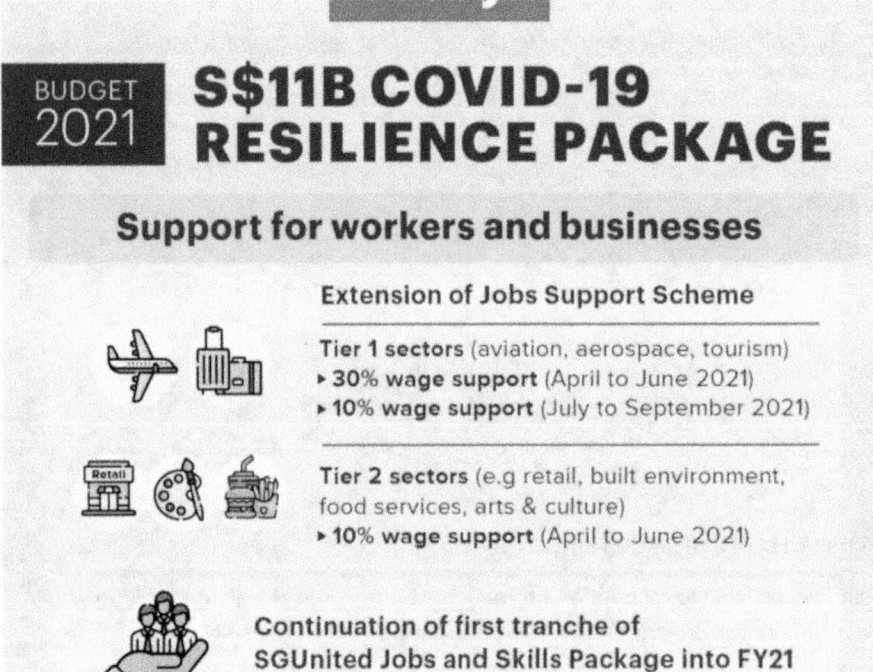

Infographic: Samuel Woo/TODAY

THE END OF SOME RELIEF SCHEMES

- Working capital loan for small- and -medium-sized companies under the Enterprise Financing Scheme (ends March 31, 2021)

- Deferment of loan and insurance premium payouts for individuals (ends June 30, 2021)

- Loan deferment for businesses (ends either March 31 or June 30, 2021, depending on the sector)

- Covid-19 Support Grant (ended Dec 31, 2020)

- Self-Employed Person Income Relief Scheme (ended Dec 31, 2020)

With respect to the last two schemes, the Government had announced in December last year a new Covid-19 Recovery Grant to support workers, including self-employed persons, who lost their jobs or experienced significant income loss.

Applications started on Jan 18 and can be made until Dec 31.

Commentary

Economic growth refers to actual (short-term) or potential (long-term) increase in goods and services produced in a country, measured as a rise in gross domestic product (GDP). Because Singapore's economy in 2022 is "projected to [unevenly] grow between 4% and 6%" among the sectors after pandemic, the government implemented S$11 billion COVID-19 Resilience Package to "address Singapore's immediate needs to safeguard public health and to provide targeted support to workers and sectors." Such expanded government expenditure is expansionary fiscal policy intended to encourage economic growth by increasing aggregate demand (AD), the total amount of real output demanded at different price levels in a given period, and by reducing cyclical unemployment, job losses due to insufficient AD during economic contraction (recession). This commentary's conceptual focus is economic well-being, the quality of living standards. Unevenly distributed growth between economic sectors and involved workers in Singapore implies disparities in the present and future economic well-being, hence the stable financial abilities to fulfill human needs, make personal economic choices, and maintain adequate income levels in the long-term.

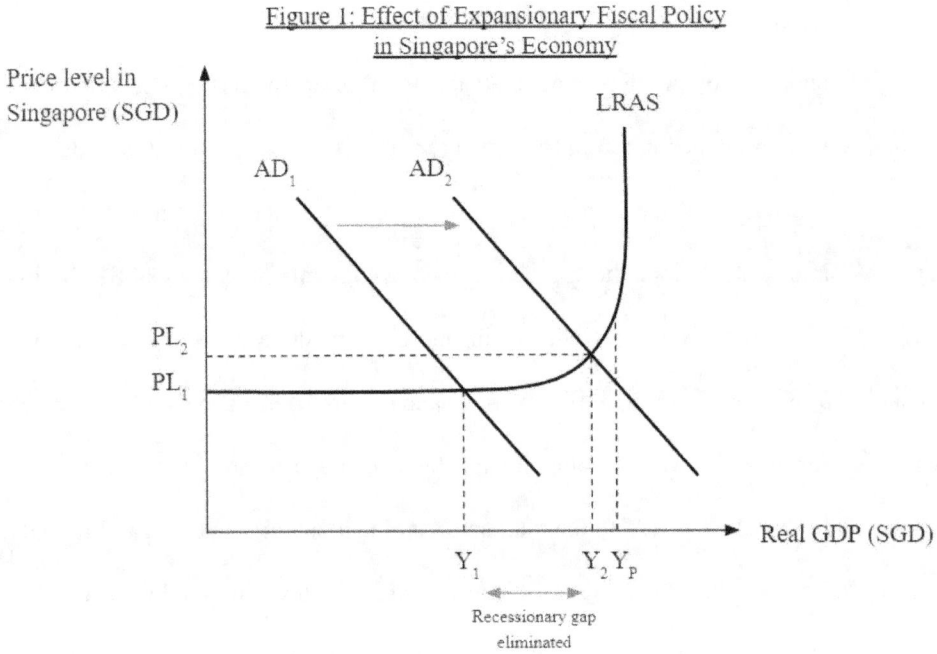

Figure 1 shows general level of economic activity expanded through Singapore's expansionary fiscal policy. As consumption, investment, government spending, and net exports are determinants of AD, increases in Singaporean government's spending directly lead to its rightward shift from AD_1 to AD_2. This further increases the price level from PL_1 to PL_2 to satisfy higher demand. Real GDP also increases from Y_1 to Y_2, reducing recessionary gap ($Y_2 - Y_1$) and approaching the potential GDP (Y_P) while achieving the government's macroeconomic objective of economic growth.

Resilience Package provides support for "sectors that are still affected by the economic disruption [from] the global pandemic," which includes companies and self-employed individuals in aerospace, tourism, retail, food services, sports, and arts. Fiscal policy's such ability to target sectors according to government priorities is critical in effectively reducing the disparities of actual growth in Singapore. In the long-run for sectors growing at a steady rate, this also assures economic sustainability by preventing inflation; price increases due to production capacity being considerably greater than demand.

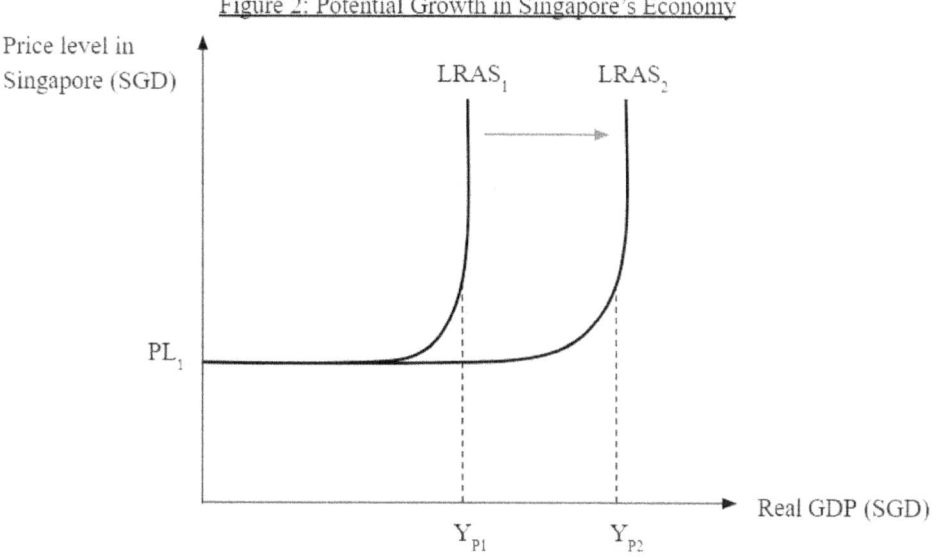

Figure 2: Potential Growth in Singapore's Economy

Shown by the outward shift of LRAS and an increase in Y_P from Y_{P1} to Y_{P2}, figure 2 exhibits Singapore's potential economic growth on account of domestic firms' and workers' welfare.

Businesses benefit from selected government spending on Job Support Scheme. Additional funds available for employment offer incentives to invest in research and development, which enhances current technologies, resulting in improved productivity and efficiency. This would promote a stable economic environment for potential growth. Moreover, if firms reduce the price of products following higher investment, their international competitiveness would arise.

The policy's wage subsidies in SGUnited Jobs and Skills Package advantage various citizens, which includes fresh graduates, ex-offenders, mid-career or older workers, and disabled or unemployed individuals. As businesses allocate more labour resources by creating "200000 jobs and 35000 training opportunities," the country's cyclical unemployment falls and households benefit as their disposable income increases. Consumers are also favoured with increased consumer confidence through stabilized unemployment rates. At the same time, human capital and labour productivity improve, causing a higher GDP and potential growth. This is beneficial for the entire Singaporean society as it indicates higher living standards, promoting economic well-being.

Nevertheless, a constraint of expansionary fiscal policy is that the government's high expenditure of a total of S$11 billion cannot be sustained in the long-run. Particularly because of time delays until the policy takes effect, budget deficit and debt can arise when government spending on Resilience Package is greater than revenue. Increased borrowing may also cause higher interest rates, possibly crowding out private investment from businesses and investors, which is the opposite of Singapore's objective to raise AD. However, tax revenues from recovered firms and newly employed workers could outweigh costs for the government over an extended period. Furthermore, the government is worse off for opportunity costs that may hinder other areas of spending such as public goods (infrastructure and education), lowering overall economic well-being of the citizens.

In addition to expansionary fiscal policy, Singapore could implement other demand-side policies as higher AD increases GDP and cures cyclical unemployment. Expansionary monetary policy, adopted by central bank to encourage consumption and investment, and expand money supply by decreasing interest rates, is an example. This does not raise problems of time lags and high government expenditure; however, specific sectors cannot be targeted and low consumer and business confidence during recession may not increase AD to sufficient levels.

Unprecedented instability and uncertainties brought by COVID-19 pandemic necessitate various approaches. Fiscal stimulus of increased government spending advantages most stakeholders while decreasing unemployment and improving economic well-being of households by reducing the gaps of actual growth in Singapore. If Resilience Package is effectively carried out, economic growth will be achieved, but a combination of both demand-side measures may be unavoidable for sustainable long-term recovery.

Unit of the syllabus	The global economy
Title of the article	"China lowers tariffs to boost high-quality growth, high-level opening-up"
Source of the article	https://www.bignewsnetwork.com/news/27201682 2/china-lowers-tariffs-to-boost-high-quality-growth-high-level-opening-up
Date the article was published	21 December 2021
Date the article was accessed	4 February 2022
Date the commentary was written	8 February 2022
Key concept	Interdependence
Word count	800

:]BIG NEWS NETWORK

≡

China lowers tariffs to boost high-quality growth, high-level opening-up

© Provided by Xinhua

BEIJING, Dec. 24 (Xinhua) -- A sweeping number of import items will enjoy lower tariffs next year as China has made new tariff adjustments for trade pacts, soon to take effect, amid efforts to improve the quality of life and boost opening up.

The Customs Tariff Commission of the State Council announced earlier this month to implement provisional tariffs that are lower than the most-favored-nation rates on 954 imported commodities starting Jan. 1, 2022. The figure saw an increase from 883 last year and 859 in 2019.

"Many of the imports on the list are heavily featured in people's daily lives so that foreign firms can benefit from China's development," said Mei Xinyu, a researcher with the Chinese Academy of International Trade and Economic Cooperation under the Ministry of Commerce.

The country will also grant zero-tariff treatment on 98 percent of taxable items originating in the least-developed countries, according to the commission.

AIMING FOR HIGH QUALITY

According to experts and industry insiders, imports included in the adjustments tell tales of improving livelihood and industrial upgrade aimed at low-carbon outcomes, both traits of high-quality growth.

Tariffs on medical products such as a new cancer drug and artificial joints have been lowered -- a continuation of similar moves in recent years to reduce medical costs and bolster public health.

Since 2018, China has either exempted or lowered tariffs on two batches of cancer drugs, artificial cardiac valves and hearing aids.

Tariffs on some aquatic products, baby clothing, artworks, ski gear are slashed to accommodate consumer demand for quality lifestyles and winter sports, said the commission.

The 954 products also include auto parts that help cut greenhouse gas emissions, as well as high-voltage cables for high-speed trains and fuel-cell components that are expected to bolster high-tech manufacturing.

Meanwhile, the average tariff rate on 62 products of information technology will be slashed from 3.4 percent to 1.7 percent starting July 1, 2022.

These moves will help keep domestic industrial and supply chains stable, spur innovations and industrial upgrade, as well as advance low-carbon development, analysts and industry insiders say.

HIGH-LEVEL OPENING UP

The new adjustments follow China's overriding trend of tariff reduction in the past two decades. The country has cut its overall tariff rate from 15.3 percent in 2001 to 9.8 percent in 2010 to fulfill its accession commitment to the World Trade Organization (WTO), before bringing it further down to 7.4 percent currently.

In latest efforts toward high-level opening up, China will impose conventional tariff rates on some products from 29 countries and regions in accordance with relevant trade agreements and preferential arrangements, resulting in lower tariffs on products from countries including New Zealand, Peru, Switzerland, Pakistan, Mauritius, and Costa Rica.

The country also introduced lower or zero tariffs in accordance with trade agreements under the Regional Comprehensive Economic Partnership (RCEP) and the new free trade agreement between China and Cambodia, both to come into effect beginning 2022.

While China had already made tariff cuts with certain members of the RCEP, the 2022 adjustments covered more products, showcasing China's commitment to tariff arrangements under the world's largest free trade agreement, said Cui Fan, a professor at the University of International Business and Economics.

"China's compliance to trade rules under the RCEP will help advance China's high-level opening up, and in turn boost the integration of industrial, supply and value chains between the RCEP members, injecting impetus into world economic recovery," said Cui.

Under the RCEP, China and Japan will see the first bilateral tariff cuts in the form of zero-tariff treatment on 24.9 percent of imported items from Japan and 55.5 percent of imported items from China in 2022. Companies from both sides are expected to benefit from the agreement.

Experts say that China's current overall tariff level, which is nearing that of many developed countries and still decreasing, will help facilitate global trade with lower costs.

In the first three quarters of the year, China's merchandise imports accounted for around 12 percent of the world's total, up from 11.54 percent in 2020, according to WTO data. Its foreign trade value expanded 22 percent year on year to 35.39 trillion yuan (about 5.56 trillion U.S. dollars) in the January-November period.

China has vowed to expand high-quality and institutional opening-up, grant foreign-funded enterprises national treatment, attract more investment from multinational companies, and facilitate the early implementation of major foreign-invested projects in 2022, according to the tone-setting annual Central Economic Work Conference early this month.

To that end, China is working on a slew of measures on top of tariff reductions like shortening the negative list for foreign investment and introducing a negative list for cross-border services trade in the country's free trade zones.

Commentary

An economy's increased gross domestic product, value of produced goods and services, results in economic growth. Trade liberalization involves removing barriers like tariffs, taxes imposed on imports, to ease and encourage free trade between nations. In domestic country, tariff removal decreases the price and makes imports desirable and competitive.

The article addresses Chinese government's proposal to "implement provisional tariffs [...] on 954 imported commodities" that are "heavily featured in people's daily lives," which will "improve quality of life and boost opening up" while allowing "foreign firms [to] benefit from China's development." In response, foreign exporters, Chinese producers and consumers, and their governments all interact to different degrees. Thus, the key concept of interdependence, the interactions between economic actors within and across nations to attain objectives and growth, is incorporated in this commentary.

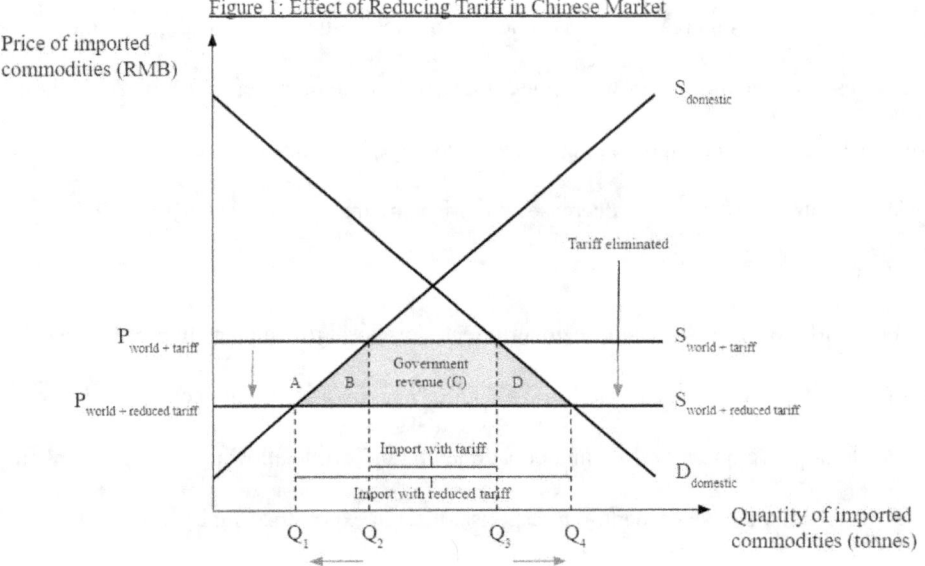
Figure 1: Effect of Reducing Tariff in Chinese Market

Figure 1 exhibits the effect of tariff reduction in Chinese market, involving domestic demand ($D_{domestic}$) and supply ($S_{domestic}$). With reduced costs of export, foreign exporters provide higher quantity of goods ($Q_4 - Q_1$) at lower price ($P_{world+reduced\ tariff}$) as the movement ($P_{world+tariff} \rightarrow P_{world+reduced\ tariff}$). This allows additional revenue $P_{world+reduced\ tariff} \cdot (Q_4 - Q_1)$ rather than $P_{world+tariff} \cdot (Q_3 - Q_2)$. Consequently, quantity demanded for imports increases from Q_3 to Q_4 and Chinese consumers' surplus increases by A+B+C+D as they are willing and able to purchase higher quantity (Q_4) at lower price ($P_{world+reduced\ tariff}$). Because Chinese producers are unable to compete with foreign producers, quantity supplied domestically decreases from Q_2 to Q_1 as the movement ($S_{world+tariff} \rightarrow S_{world+reduced\ tariff}$). This results in their surplus decrease A. Similarly, Chinese government's revenue C = tariff $\cdot (Q_3 - Q_2)$ is removed with reduced tariff. Although a complete elimination is unattainable, resource misallocation from inefficient domestic producers, thus welfare loss for society, is also partially decreased by B+D; Chinese and global economy become more efficient.

Through interdependence, Chinese government's decision to reduce tariffs generates varying economic consequences for other interacting stakeholders of economy.

82

Firstly, Chinese consumers dependent on selective consumption benefit from greater choice. A wider variety of commodities supplied by producers in exporting countries will "[accommodate demand for quality lifestyles and winter sports]," "[reduce] medical costs and [bolster] public health" for domestic consumers. This enables households of all income levels to enjoy a higher quantity of goods of leisure, health, and basic needs at lower price, relieving burden and boosting domestic economic activity, which implies economic well-being.

Secondly, Chinese producers are disadvantaged with decreased sales at any given price as they cannot compete with lower-cost foreign producers. Yet, shortage of resources caused by factory closure and unemployment during pandemic could be alleviated with imported goods, favouring domestic industries to utilize them at lower price and achieve greater efficiency with improved quantity and quality of secondary products. As argued by analysts, tariff-lowered commodities will "keep domestic industrial and supply chains stable, spur innovations and industrial upgrade, as well as advance low-carbon development." This alludes sustainable economic growth for firms dependent on cheaper imports.

Thirdly, the global economy and its interdependent nations and grow economically through globalization. As more imports are demanded from China, bigger labour force is created in foreign markets, allocating employment in the entire economy. Furthermore, intensifying of trade liberalization encourages worldwide economic activity, expanding markets and providing economies of scale for firms. Subsequently, increased competition incentivizes them to invest in technology and improve efficiency. The anticipated "foreign-funded enterprises national treatment" and "investment from multinational companies" in China will also increase the quantity and quality of products, indicating economic growth. International relation between 29 partnering countries and RCEP members will also enhance "in accordance with relevant trade agreements and preferential arrangements," eventually allowing China to consolidate their position as the leading economy along with "many developed countries." However, nations not involved in such agreements are disadvantaged and discriminated as their share of world imports and exports decrease with limited access to the protectionism measures of trade liberalization. This restrains global scale trades and deteriorates resource misallocation in the long-term.

While Chinese government is worsened by revenue loss from decreased tariffs, China does not rely heavily on imports as one of the largest exporting countries, and tariffs are not a primary government revenue source. Moreover, exceedingly increased imports $(Q_3 - Q_2 \rightarrow Q_4 - Q_1)$ and resulting tariff costs are likely to compensate a portion of the loss. Nonetheless, the government should assure the extent to which domestic markets can manage the impacts of lowered tariffs along with the effects to national production as the principal objective is to encourage long-term recovery from pandemic. Internalized protectionism like expansionary fiscal policies that support specific sectors requiring assistance would stimulate economic growth without harming local industries.

Overall, through the interdependence of all stakeholders, tariff reduction that leads to greater efficiency and international solidarity is projected to promote Chinese and global economic growth by implicating employment and well-being.

3. PORTFOLIO THREE

Commentary 1

Title of the article: *Delhi imposes 70% 'corona tax' on alcohol to deter large crowds*

Source of the article: Reuters
https://www.reuters.com/article/us-health-coronavirus-india-idUSKBN22H0NB

Date the article was published: May 5, 2020

Date the commentary was written: April 14, 2021

Word count of the commentary: 792 words

Unit of the syllabus to which the article relates: Microeconomics

Key concept being used: Intervention

MONEY NEWS

MAY 5, 2020 / 3:19 PM / UPDATED 1 YEAR AGO

Delhi imposes 70% 'corona tax' on alcohol to deter large crowds

By Sanjeev Miglani, Nidhi Verma   f   y

NEW DELHI (Reuters) - Officials in India's capital imposed a special tax of 70% on retail liquor purchases from Tuesday, to deter large gatherings at stores as authorities ease a six-week lockdown imposed to slow the spread of the coronavirus.

Slideshow (3 images)

Taxes on alcohol are a key contributor to the revenue of many of India's 36 states and federal territories, most of which are running short of funds because of the lengthy disruption in economic activity caused by the virus.

Police baton-charged hundreds of people who had flocked to liquor shops when they opened on Monday for the first time in a relaxation of the world's biggest lockdown, which is set to run until May 17.

The Delhi state government announced the "special corona fee" in a public notice late on Monday.

"It was unfortunate that chaos was seen at some shops in Delhi," said Arvind Kejriwal, the state's chief minister.

"If we come to know about violations of social distancing and other norms from any area, then we will have to seal the area and revoke the relaxations there," he added.

Other states, such as southern Andhra Pradesh, where people also violated social distancing measures to queue up in their hundreds for alcohol, also hiked prices.

The increases come as India reported 3,900 new infections on Tuesday for its highest single day rise, taking the tally to 46,432. The death toll stood at 1,568, the health ministry said.

Health experts said the daily increase shows India remains at risk despite a severe lockdown that has confined its population of 1.3 billion to their homes since late March, with all public transport halted and economic activity nearly frozen.

"The curve has not shown a downward trend. That is cause for concern," said Dr Randeep Guleria, director of New Delhi's premier All-India Institute of Medical Sciences.

India's average daily increase in cases has been 6.1 over the past week, behind Russia and Brazil but higher than Britain, the United States and Italy.

The biggest spikes were recorded in the western states of Maharashtra, home to India's commercial capital of Mumbai, and Gujarat as well as Delhi. These densely populated urban centres drive India's economy, powered by armies of migrant workers.

Government officials said the lockdown had helped avert a surge of infections that could have overwhelmed medical services, however.

Now cases are doubling every 12 days, up from 3.4 days when the lockdown began, said Lav Agarwal, a joint secretary in the health ministry.

"Lockdown and containment are yielding results, the challenge is now to improve on the doubling rate," he added.

(Interactive graphic tracking global spread of coronavirus: open tmsnrt.rs/3aIRuz7 in an external browser.)

Reporting by Sanjeev Miglani; Editing by Clarence Fernandez

Our Standards: The Thomson Reuters Trust Principles.

In the Reuters article, India imposes an additional 70% "corona tax" on alcohol to deter large crowds that foster COVID-19. Published on May 5th, 2020, Reuters reports the Delhi state also exhausted most government funds due to the COVID-19-induced economic shutdown.

The key concept in the article is a form of **intervention**. Traditionally, government **intervention** has two purposes: increase government revenue and decrease consumption. In this case, the state government aims to increase revenue from alcohol sales by increasing the tax. Simultaneously, consumption is reduced by the supply-demand law. This would reduce gatherings, thereby lessening instances of COVID-19 transmittance.

The Delhi government is **intervening** by levying an indirect ad valorem excise tax, a percentage Pigouvian tax on a demerit good. Any good that engenders a negative externality—a harmful side effect to a third party—is classified as a demerit. Similarly, a tax on a demerit good to minimise the negative externality is a Pigouvian tax.

As the consumers overvalue the benefit of the alcohol, a negative externality of consumption is created: the economic concept is market failure. The externality is not recognised by the users, thus requiring government **intervention**. In this case, this externality is COVID-19, with India "not showing a downward trend [in cases], with the biggest spikes in Delhi." This phenomenon is exhibited in the figure below.

Market for Alcohol in Delhi: Before Intervention

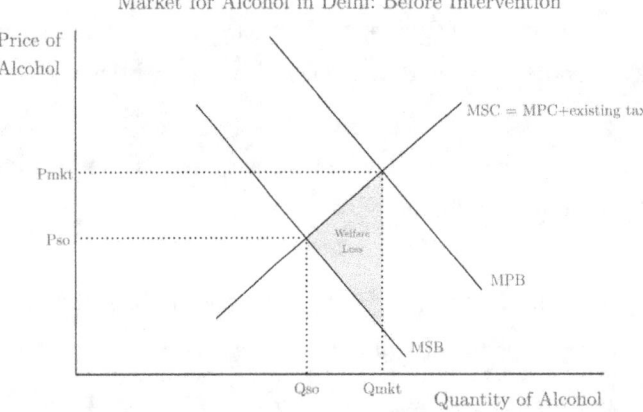

Figure 1: Market of Alcohol in Delhi, India: Before **Intervention**

The consumer's overvaluation of the product results in the Marginal Private Benefit (MPB) being larger than the Marginal Social Benefit (MSB). This creates market failure because the individual's

perceived benefit is greater than the socially optimal benefit. Another indicator of this is the area of Welfare Loss, which depicts the negative externality on goods sold above the socially optimal quantity, Qso. It is found by multiplying the amount of surplus quantity (Qmkt (market) − Qso (socially optimal)) with the surplus price (Pmkt − Pso), and evaluates lost economic efficiency. This area traditionally includes alcohol-related illness treatment costs, but in this context, it may also include COVID-19 regulation and treatment costs induced by excessive gatherings.

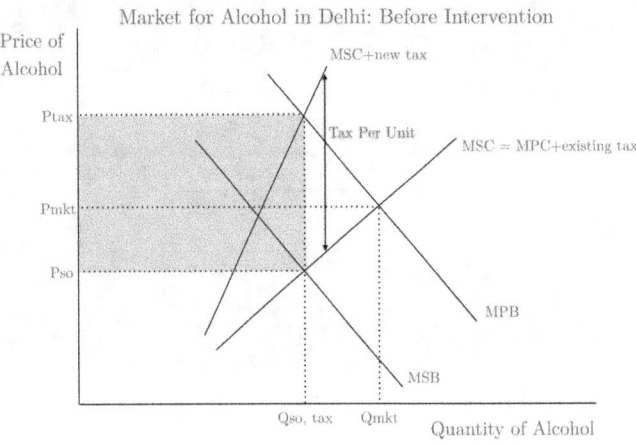

Figure 2: Market of Alcohol in Delhi, India: After **Intervention**

To fix the market failure, the government **intervened** by imposing a Pigouvian tax on alcohol. This "tax rate of 70%" results in an upward shift of MSC, changing the price to Ptax. Furthermore, the negative externality caused by the COVID-inducing gatherings is ideally internalised as the level of output decreases to Pareto Optimal (socially optimal). This means that the output at MPB has decreased to MSB, eliminating the negative externality. The area of Welfare Loss is eliminated, demonstrating efficiency.

The consumer loses consumer surplus in the short run as the price increases from Pmkt to Ptax. The producer's negative impact—induced by the quantity decrease—is lesser than the consumer's. This is because the addictive nature of alcohol renders it such that the quantity demanded is relatively unresponsive to changes in price: alcohol has an inelastic price elasticity of demand. Thus, the tax incidence on the consumer is much higher than the loss in revenue of the producer. However, society as a whole also benefits because the "[closures] averted a surge of infections."

The government also generates high revenue from the **intervention**, indicated by the area in red (Figure 2), and calculated by multiplying the quantity with the increase in price (from Pso to Ptax). It is paid entirely by the consumers, who have inelastic responses to quantity despite the high tax rate. Thus, the government gains immediate benefit through higher tax revenue as the price increase is greater than the quantity demanded decreases. Consequently, the government can reallocate this revenue—paid majorly by the consumers—for COVID-19-relief programs. This is crucial as they "are running short of funds."

Furthermore, there is a greater consumption reduction in the long run. As the price of alcohol becomes relatively high for an extended period, consumers look to save money and, with time, find alternatives. Therefore, the elasticity of demand increases as time increases the substitutability of a good. In Delhi, this results in fewer gatherings and alcohol consumption in the long run.

The **intervention** still has several key disadvantages, though. Firstly, indirect taxes are almost exclusively regressive. This means that poorer individuals pay a higher percentage of their disposable income than wealthier consumers, increasing wealth inequality. Additionally, as the PED of alcohol is low and "cases are doubling every 12 days," the primary purpose of the Delhi government to decrease consumption in the streets may not have been achieved to the desired extent in the short run. The **intervention** may be too insignificant to impact quantity as intended.

Finally, with significant consumption decreases inducing losses in revenue in the long run, producers are incentivised to release employees, leading to higher unemployment rates. This can cause many firms to exit the market due to losses.

To conclude, the key concept discussed in this commentary is **intervention**. By implementing taxes, the government has generated revenue and "contained" consumption, but there may be adverse long term effects. Furthermore, the tax could be too low to decrease consumption to the desired extent.

Word Count: 792

Title of the article: *Here's what's in Biden's infrastructure proposal*

Source of the article: CNN
https://www.cnn.com/2021/03/31/politics/infrastructure-proposal-biden-expl
ainer/index.html

Date the article was published: April 21, 2021

Date the commentary was written: December 6, 2021

Word count of the commentary: 794 words

Unit of the syllabus to which the article relates: Macroeconomics

Key concept being used: Well-being

Here's what's in Biden's infrastructure proposal

By Tami Luhby, Katie Lobosco and Kate Sullivan, CNN

Updated 1416 GMT (2216 HKT) April 21, 2021

Editor's Note: *This story originally ran on March 31 and has been updated with new developments.*

(CNN) — Now that his massive coronavirus relief package is law, President Joe Biden is laying out his next big proposal: A roughly $2 trillion plan for improving the nation's infrastructure and shifting to greener energy over the next 8 years.

Related Article: With an eye on history, Biden moves on big, bold and progressive infrastructure package

The nation's infrastructure is sorely in need of repair. It recently earned a C- score from the American Society of Civil Engineers, which said an additional $2.6 trillion in funding is required over the next decade. But Biden is also pitching his plan as an investment to benefit communities of color, rural Americans and others burdened by decay or lagging modernization.

He unveiled the effort, dubbed the American Jobs Plan, at a March event in Pittsburgh, Pennsylvania -- the opening move in what's expected to be a months-long negotiation with Congress.

The infrastructure spending plan is the first of a two-part proposal to help the nation's economy recover from the coronavirus pandemic. The President is expected to unveil his package focusing on the "care economy," including investments in education and child care, in coming weeks.

The President plans to pay for this part of his recovery package by raising corporate taxes -- a core campaign promise the administration says would raise more than $2 trillion over the next 15 years.

Here's what we know so far about Biden's infrastructure proposal, according to the White House.

Transportation: $621 billion

Contractors work on a portion of Highway 101 in Petaluma, California, on March 22. Improving roads and bridges is a key part of Biden's infrastructure plan.

Funding improvements to roads, bridges, railways and other infrastructure has been a central piece of Biden's recovery plans. He has said that it will create "really good-paying jobs" and help the nation compete better.

Biden would spend $621 billion on roads, bridges, public transit, rail, ports, waterways, airports and electric vehicles in service of improving air quality, reducing congestion and limiting greenhouse gas emissions.

His proposal calls for allocating $115 billion to modernize 20,000 miles of highways, roads and main streets, and $20 billion to improve road safety for all users. It would fix the "most economically significant large bridges" and repair the worst 10,000 smaller bridges.

Biden would also invest $85 billion to modernize existing transit and help agencies expand their systems to meet demand. This would double federal funding for public transit.

Related Article: Buttigieg says no gas or mileage tax in Biden's infrastructure plan

Another $80 billion would go to address Amtrak's repair backlog and modernize the Northeast Corridor line between Boston and Washington DC -- the line Biden relied on for decades to get home to Delaware -- as well as to connect more cities.

Biden's plan would help modernize Amtrak and repair railways.

Also, the President would funnel $25 billion to airports and $17 billion to inland waterways, ports and ferries.

Biden is also proposing to accelerate the shift to electric vehicles with a $174 billion investment in the electric vehicle market. It includes giving consumers rebates and tax incentives to buy American-made electric vehicles and establishing grant and incentive programs to build a national network of 500,000 charging stations by 2030. It would also replace 50,000 diesel transit vehicles and electrify at least 20% of yellow school buses.

Home care services and workforce: $400 billion

Biden would provide $400 billion to bolster caregiving for aging and disabled Americans.

His plan would expand access to long-term care services under Medicaid, eliminating the wait list for hundreds of thousands of people. It would provide more opportunity for people to receive care at home through community-based services or from family members.

It would also improve the wages of home health workers, who now make approximately $12 an hour. One in six live in poverty, the administration says. It would put in place an infrastructure to give caregiving workers the opportunity to join a union.

During his presidential campaign, Biden said he would devote $450 billion to allow more older Americans and their families to receive care at home or in their communities, as opposed to nursing homes and other institutions.

Manufacturing: $300 billion

Employees work inside a semiconductor manufacturing facility in Malta, New York, on March 16, 2021. Production plants for semiconductors have become a focal point of economic recovery.

Biden wants to put $300 billion toward boosting manufacturing.

Under his plan, $50 billion of the money would be invested in semiconductor manufacturing and another $30 billion would go towards medical manufacturing to help shore up the nation's ability to respond to a future outbreak.

Some of the funds would be carved out for manufacturers that focus on clean energy, rural communities, and programs that give small businesses access to credit. About $20 billion would be used to create regional innovation hubs that would support community-led projects.

Biden is asking Congress to include $46 billion that would be used to make federal purchases of things like electric cars, charging ports, and electric heat pumps for housing and commercial buildings that would boost the clean energy industry.

Biden has already signed an executive order aimed at boosting American manufacturing. It set in motion a process that would change the rules regarding federal spending on American-made goods, equipment, vehicles and materials for infrastructure projects -- with a 180-day deadline that comes up in July.

Housing: $213 billion

A construction worker walks through an affordable housing project in Oakland, California, in 2019. Biden's plan would invest in affordable housing.

The plan would invest $213 billion toward building, renovating and retrofitting more than two million homes and housing units.

Biden is calling on Congress to produce, preserve and retrofit more than a million affordable and energy efficient housing units. The plan would also build and rehabilitate more than 500,000 homes for low- and middle-income homebuyers.

The proposal would eliminate exclusionary zoning laws, which the White House says inflates housing and construction costs. Biden is calling on Congress to enact a new grant program that awards flexible funding to jurisdictions that take steps to eliminate barriers to creating affordable housing.

Homes would be upgraded though block grant programs, extending and expanding home and commercial efficiency tax credits and through the Weatherization Assistance Program.

Research and development: $180 billion

Biden is calling on Congress to invest $180 billion to advance US leadership in critical technologies, upgrade the US's research infrastructure and establish the US as a leader in climate science, innovation and research and development.

His plan would also aim to eliminate racial and gender inequities in research and development and science, technology, engineering and math. Biden is calling on Congress to make research and development investments in historically Black colleges and other minority-serving institutions.

Water: $111 billion

Workers in Flint, Michigan, prepare to replace a lead water service line pipe in 2016. Biden's plan aims to replace all of the nation's lead pipes and services lines.

Biden's plan allocates $111 billion to rebuild the country's water infrastructure.

It would replace all of the nation's lead pipes and service lines in order to improve the health of American children and communities of color. The White House says replacing the pipes would reduce lead exposure in 400,000 schools and childcare facilities.

The proposal would upgrade the country's drinking water, wastewater and stormwater systems, tackle new contaminants and support clean water infrastructure in rural parts of the country.

Schools: $100 billion

Biden calls for $100 billion to build new public schools and upgrade existing buildings with better ventilation systems, updated technology labs, and improved school kitchens that can prepare more nutritious meals.

Another $12 billion would go to states to use towards infrastructure needs at community colleges.

The President is calling for an additional $25 billion to help upgrade child care facilities and increase the supply of child care in areas that need it the most. The plan also calls for expand a tax credit to encourage employers to build care facilities at places of work.

Digital infrastructure: $100 billion

A data tower in Lowell, Ohio, was updated in February to provide broadband access to the surrounding area. Biden wants to provide every American with access to affordable high-speed internet.

Biden wants to invest $100 billion in order to give every American access to affordable, reliable and high-speed broadband.

The proposal would build a high-speed broadband infrastructure in order to reach 100% coverage across the nation. The plan would aim to promote transparency and competition among internet providers.

Biden says he is committed to working with Congress to reduce the cost of broadband internet and increase its adoption in both rural and urban areas.

Workforce development: $100 billion

The President would allocate $100 billion to workforce development -- helping dislocated workers, assisting underserved groups and getting students on career paths before they graduate high school.

It would provide $40 billion to retrain dislocated workers in high-demand sectors, such as clean energy, manufacturing and caregiving.

It would invest $12 billion in programs to train the formerly incarcerated, create a new subsidized jobs program, eliminate sub-minimum wage provisions and support community violence prevention programs.

The proposal would also funnel $48 billion into apprenticeships, career pathway programs for middle and high school students and job training programs at community colleges.

Veterans' hospitals and federal buildings: $18 billion

The plan would provide $18 billion to modernize the Veterans Affairs' hospitals, which are on average more than 40 years older than a private sector hospital, according to the White House.

It also calls for $10 billion to modernize federal buildings.

Corporate tax hike: Biden would raise the corporate income tax rate to 28%, up from 21%. The rate had been as high as 35% before former President Donald Trump and congressional Republicans cut taxes in 2017.

Global minimum tax: The proposal would increase the minimum tax on US corporations to 21% and calculate it on a country-by-country basis to deter companies from sheltering profits in international tax havens.

Tax on book income: The President would levy a 15% minimum tax on the income the largest corporations report to investors, known as book income, as opposed to the income reported to the Internal Revenue Service.

Corporate inversions: Biden would make it harder for US companies to acquire or merge with a foreign business to avoid paying US taxes by claiming to be a foreign company. And he wants to encourage other countries to adopt strong minimum taxes on corporations, including by denying certain deductions to foreign companies based in countries without such a tax.

In the article from CNN, titled, "Here's what's in Biden's infrastructure proposal," the President of the United States proposes a US$ 2 trillion plan to address infrastructure and education concerns in the economy. Published on April 21st, 2021, CNN reports that this plan is mainly focused on poverty-stricken areas.

The key concept in the article is **well-being**. Biden aims to improve infrastructure and quality of education in communities "in need of repair". To do this, he will use expansionary supply-side interventionist policy (government funding into supply-side factors)—consequently, the long-run productivity of businesses and quality of labor increases. Likewise, real long-run output as measured by Gross Domestic Product (GDP) will increase. As GDP also measures standards of living, this policy also deals with the **well-being** of American citizens.

Biden cites that supply must "meet the demand," suggesting that spare capacity—available factors of production—is exhausted in the economy. Any further demand increases would increase inflation as output is near its maximum. This phenomenon is exhibited in the figure below:

Market of the United States Before Policy

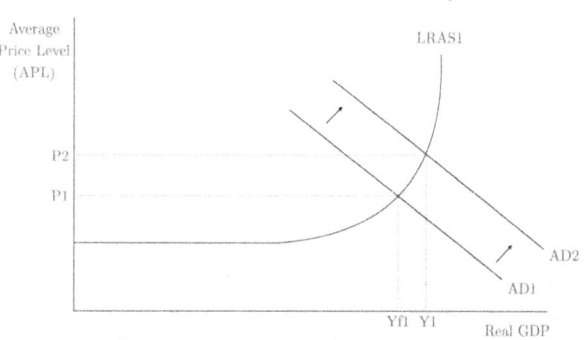

Figure 1: Aggregate Market of the United States: Before Policy

The initial increase in aggregate demand that "supply must meet" causes inflation. As spare capacity is exhausted, AD2 increases average price levels from P1 to P2. Due to decreases in purchasing power due to inflation, workers eventually demand higher wages as their real income decreases. Subsequently, firms oblige, increasing costs of factors of production. This further increases the rate of inflation, yet again encouraging workers to demand higher wages. This process is called an inflationary spiral wherein the level of output does not change: only the level of inflation increases. This process systematically reduces the real GDP per capita in the United States, decreasing **well-**

being.

To address concerns in the economy, the President is proposing an interventionist supply-side policy to boost the long-run aggregate supply curve (see figure below).

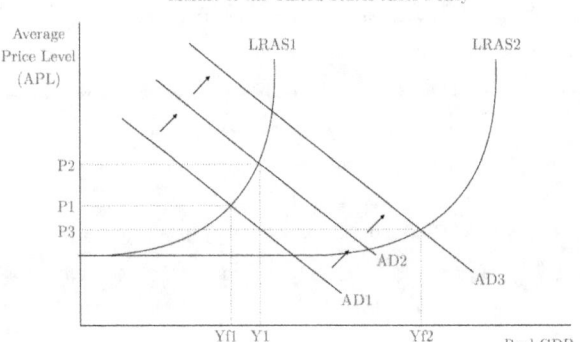

Figure 2: Aggregate Market of the United States: After Policy

The policy corresponds to a shift of the LRAS curve to the right in Figure 2 as the maximum level of sustainable output increases. This is because inflation decreases and real GDP per capita rises— better **well-being** for the average individual. The price level drops from P2 to P3 in the figure, while output increases from Y1 to Yf2. As there is a significant increase in government spending to fund the supply-side policy, the aggregate demand increases to AD3. This explains why Yf2 is larger than the intersection of AD2 and LRAS2. The price levels remain lower than P1, though, as LRAS2 increases spare capacity. Implicitly, this increase in real GDP catalyzes the accelerator effect in firms. With promises of "boosting American manufacturing," all-time high business confidence would encourage firms to invest more. As investment is a determinant of aggregate demand, the supply-side policy also boosts demand. This, along with increasing economic growth, could help offset the uncertainty surrounding "infrastructure in sore need of repair" in the United States, which could also be inhibiting investment, productivity and **well-being**.

The effectiveness of the policy depends heavily on whether the government has chosen the 'right' infrastructure to invest in. For instance, investment into education and training could offer better economic output and, thus, **well-being** increases than home care services. Interventionist policy always inherently involves opportunity cost as governments have access to limited resources and face the consequences of budget deficits. Thus, policymakers must ensure government expenditure is allocated as efficiently as possible.

Another limitation lies in how Biden is funding the policy. By increasing corporate tax rates from 21% to 28%, there could be a decrease in output and an increase in price levels as firms' costs rise. This would both increase unemployment and inflation, thereby decreasing **well-being**, negating benefits of the supply-side policy. Moreover, it would also decrease businesses' incentive to invest in the quality and quantity of factors of production as their disposable income—available income after taxes—decreases. Ultimately, this has a direct, negative effect on the long-run aggregate supply. Fundamentally, it is counter-intuitive to fund expansionary policy through contractionary policy.

Furthermore, if Biden's expenditures exceed revenue from the taxes, the government would effectively be deficit spending. Prolonged deficit spending could lead to unsustainable levels of debt and, catastrophically, defaults. This outcome can cause a higher cost of loans and harm growth rates and investment.

The success of this policy also depends heavily on the extent of time lag. Investment into education, training and transportation often takes decades to make an impact. The corollary is that it may be too slow to counteract the current inflationary pressure and decrease **well-being** despite the high costs. Government policy is also intrinsically inflexible; it is morally and politically difficult for a government to reduce welfare programs or infrastructure funding.

Ultimately, Biden should be cautious, ensuring that the policy is net-positive in the long run. If well-directed and effectively timed, an interventionist policy is a necessary strategy to reduce inflation and increase output.

Word Count: 794

Commentary 3

Title of the article: *EU imposes tariffs on stainless steel from India, Indonesia*

Source of the article: CNA
https://www.channelnewsasia.com/business/eu-imposes-tariffs-stainless-steel-india-indonesia-2323736

Date the article was published: November 19, 2021

Date the commentary was written: March 4, 2022

Word count of the commentary: 799 words

Unit of the syllabus to which the article relates: Global

Key concept being used: Interdependence

Business

EU imposes tariffs on stainless steel from India, Indonesia

FILE PHOTO: An employee works inside a stainless-steel utensil manufacturing unit on the outskirts of Jammu February 28, 2011. REUTERS/Mukesh Gupta/File Photo

19 Nov 2021 01:19AM | (Updated: 19 Nov 2021 01:14AM)

BRUSSELS : The European Union has imposed tariffs on imports of cold-rolled flat stainless steel products from India and Indonesia after an investigation found they were being sold at artificially low prices.

The European Commission, which conducted the investigation, has set duties of 10.2per cent for Indonesia's IRNC and 20.2per cent for other Indonesian producers, the EU official journal said on Thursday.

107

In the article from CNA, titled, "[European Union] imposes tariffs on stainless steel from India, Indonesia," an investigative commission found that they were being sold at artificially low prices. Published on November 19th, 2021, the article reports that the EU has placed anti-dumping measures.

The key concept in the article is **interdependence**, which is essentially a system by which two nations support each other, be it through trade, labor specialization, or capital movement. The European Commission looks to remedy the damage caused to "EU producers such as Acerinox and Outokumpu." To do this, the EU placed tariffs—a type of tax on trade—ranging from 10% to 35% on all Indian and Indonesian producers. Simultaneously, this will weaken the relationship between all countries involved, indicating a decrease in **interdependence**.

Before the protectionist measures, dumping—the sale of stainless steel at artificially low prices in the EU—by Indonesian and Indian manufacturers, caused the world price Pw to be lower than the domestic price Pd. This is depicted in the graph below.

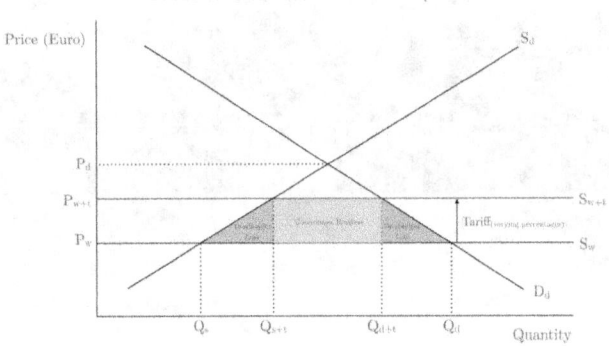

Figure 1: The Market for Stainless Steel in the European Union

At the world price, Pw, the domestic quantity demanded is Qd, but the quantity supplied by domestic producers is only Qs. Hence, the excess goods demanded by consumers, Qd – Qs, is met through imports.

In an anti-dumping effort, a tariff is imposed on imported goods by the EU. This tariff shifts the world supply curve up. The value of the tariffs varies depending on the Indonesian and Indian firms, ranging from 10% to 35%, so an exact value of tariff cannot be depicted on Figure 1.

In any case, the price of the stainless steel goods increases from Pw to P_{w+t}. As such, domestic quantity demanded decreases to Q_{d+t}. Effectively, imports also fall from $Qd - Qs$ to $Q_{d+t} - Q_{s+t}$. This fall in imports protects European producers from predatory dumping by Indonesian and Indian producers. The corollary is that domestic producers' supply increases by $Q_{s+t} - Qs$ units, increasing domestic steel industry employment. Infant—and previously less efficient—European steel firms can grow in the market. Through economies of scale, wherein increases in their quantity supplied decreases their supply cost-per-unit, they can compete without needing a tariff in the future. Also, as relatively efficient firms cannot compete in the market when dumping occurs, this policy is crucial to protect domestic producers.

With that being said, it is difficult to gauge whether international producers are dumping, even though the European commission's investigation found evidence of "artificially low prices." These international producers may be selling under domestic EU prices, but this does not mean they are selling under their production costs. The cheaper steel production in Indonesia and India may derive from their lower labor costs, economies of scale made possible by their large markets, or even subsidies—all of which explain the "artificially low prices". Hence, their lower prices may represent efficiency rather than dumping. In this case, this tariff would be detrimental to global welfare, and efficient allocation of resources. The area of welfare loss caused by the tariff is depicted in Figure 1 by the second red triangle. Additionally, all nations involved would see a decrease in **interdependence**, which is unfavorable because **interdependence** is a consequence of specialization and comparative advantage. Hence, a decrease in **interdependence** demonstrates a decrease in overall economic efficiency.

As a matter of fact, the many benefits of **interdependence** are undermined by this tariff. As countries specialize in specific sectors and trade goods they are competitively advantageous in, they gain a surplus. However, upon placing a tariff, resources are wasted on inefficient domestic firms as competitiveness in the market decreases. These could have otherwise been allocated to a comparatively advantageous EU industry, and goods could have been traded with Indonesia or China instead. Furthermore, this tariff will induce a decrease in EU consumer surplus—which is initially caused by trade and **interdependence**—depicted by the first red triangle in Figure 1. Consumer choice also decreases as goods become more expensive in the market. Moreover, with a loss in **interdependence**, Indonesia and India have reason to retaliate with their own tariffs. In this case, trade wars may ensure that permanently damage the relationship and **interdependence** between the EU and Indonesia and India.

Despite these decreases in efficiency, welfare, and **interdependence**, increases in government revenue can negate tariff externalities. As the tax cost is borne entirely by the consumers, any imported goods bought generate revenue for the government. This revenue—depicted by the green rectangle in Figure 1—can be used for any government policy, including subsidies for domestic producers to increase their competitiveness or welfare programs to counteract the market failure induced by **interdependence** decreases and tariffs.

Ultimately, the tariff will protect EU's steel producers and laborers, increasing their quantity supplied and employment, respectively. However, this policy also detracts from **interdependence**, weakening international relationships and efficiency. As there are potentially catastrophic effects associated with the tariff's negative impact on global welfare, efficient allocation of resources, and concerns of retaliation, the EU should approach this policy with caution.

Word Count: 799

4. PORTFOLIO FOUR

Author: Anonymous
Moderated Mark: 45/45
Level: Economics HL

111

Commentary 1 cover sheet

Title of the article:	Coronavirus: UK interest rates cut to lowest level ever
Source of the article:	BBC News (Business)
Date article was published:	19 March 2020
URL of the article:	https://www.bbc.co.uk/news/business-51962982
Date article was accessed:	8 March 2021
Date commentary was written:	10 March 2021
Word count of the commentary:	796
Unit of the syllabus to which the article relates:	Unit 3: Macroeconomics
Key concept being used:	Intervention

The Bank of England has cut interest rates again in an emergency move as it tries to support the UK economy in the face of the coronavirus pandemic.

It is the second cut in interest rates in just over a week, bringing them down to 0.1% from 0.25%. Interest rates are now at the lowest ever in the Bank's 325-year history.

The Bank said it would also increase its holdings of UK government and corporate bonds by £200bn with an effort to lower the cost of borrowing.

It's a dramatic move by Andrew Bailey, who only took over from Mark Carney as Bank of England governor on Monday.

Last week, the Bank announced a 0.5% cut in rates to 0.25% and a package of measures to help businesses and individuals cope with the economic damage caused by the virus.

The move coincided with additional measures announced by Chancellor Rishi Sunak in the Budget. However, the Bank said the measures it had taken so far were not going to be enough and believed "a further package of measures was warranted".

"The spread of Covid-19 and the measures being taken to contain the virus will result in an economic shock that could be sharp and large, but should be temporary," it added.

Interest rates slashed to 0.1%

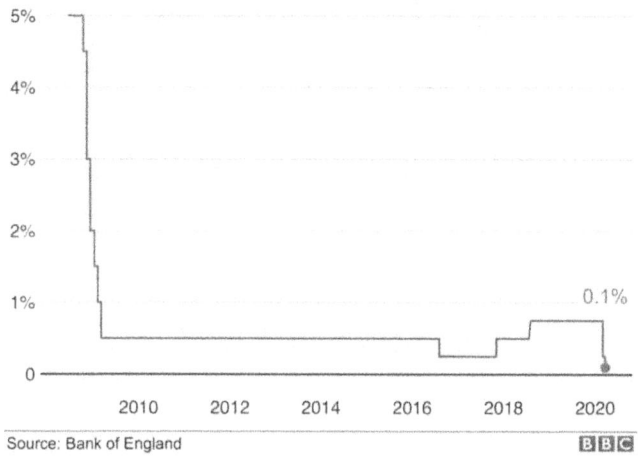

Source: Bank of England   BBC

The move comes as international investors are trying to secure more cash, in particular dollars. This means they're ditching assets such as UK government gilts, which are the "IOU" notes the government hands over to private investors willing to lend it money.

As the gilts are sold, the price drops and the yield - the effective interest rate compared to the price - rises. What that means is the cost of borrowing to private investors as well as to the government rises - just when the Bank of England wants it to fall, and the government is about to borrow huge sums. The Bank of England's plan to buy £200bn more bonds is aimed at fighting that effect.

'Lowest possible'

The fresh rate cut takes interest rates to the lowest they can feasibly go, said Jeremy Thomson-Cook, chief economist at payments company Equals Group.

"Lower rates and additional quantitative easing can keep markets satisfied and borrowing costs for both businesses and the government down but unless money is forced into the hands of small businesses soon, then it will be for nothing; they are the ones laying off staff due to a liquidity shock," he added.

Karen Ward, chief European market strategist at JPMorgan Asset Management, said: The support to the economy and health system will require vastly higher government borrowing. The central bank showing willing to buy government debt will ensure the market can absorb this additional issuance without undue stress."

The Bank of England Governor has said today's second emergency rate cut in just over a week occurred after financial markets became "borderline disorderly", with fears about coronavirus leading to a rush into the US dollar away from sterling and lending to the UK government.

"We've seen very sharp moves in financial markets in the last few days, which is the pace of which, frankly, was increasing very rapidly. And we were moving into conditions that were if not disorderly, frankly, bordering on disorderly let me put it that way," Andrew Bailey told journalists.

The Bank of England Monetary Policy Committee had an emergency call this morning so that rate cuts and further "quantitative easing" could be agreed and announced, with the Bank needing to be "on the offensive" because: "We can't wait for the hard economic data it will be too late by then", he said.

He said he had seen a range of private forecasts about the economic impact of the current crisis: "We don't have a precise forecast - every picture we look at has a very sharp V in it".

The governor also partly blamed rumours that appeared to emerge from Westminster of a shutdown to London for adding to the volatility in markets that saw sterling fall 5% against the dollar. Such a shutdown would be likely to impact on the functioning of the City.

He said: "I do have to say that, you know, there were rumours going on the market this time yesterday that there was going to be a lockdown in London. And I'd observe that did cause market prices to start moving around at that point. But I think the government has been clear, and it's clear that that is not the intention at the moment."

The governor also said that he had already intervened to try to get loans to businesses to keep people in employment, and he said the Bank had its thinking cap on as regards further monetary boosts it can make.

He reiterated his lack of enthusiasm for zero or negative interest rates because of their impact on the banking system's capacity to lend and suggested that was the reason for limiting the cut to an unusual 0.15% (rather than the usual 0.25% or 0.5%) to a record low of 0.1%.

The key Monetary Policy Committee will meet again next week.

This article discusses the Bank of England's (BoE) decision to cut interest rates to *"the[ir] lowest ever"* (0.1%) and a new quantitative easing (QE) approach to *"buy £200bn more bonds"*. These **interventionist** strategies are expansionary monetary policies, implemented by the BoE to mitigate *"economic damage"* from the Covid-19 pandemic. Expansionary monetary policy is a form of demand-side management, defined as the set of official policies governing money supply and interest rates in an economy, that aims to increase aggregate demand (AD). This commentary's key concept is **intervention**.

Figure-1 displays the economic motivation behind the BoE's **intervention** of cutting interest rates as *"an emergency move fac[ing] Covid-19"*. Interest rates refer to the base rate set by a country's central bank, which when lowered, impact the borrowing and lending within an economy: costs of borrowing and rewards for saving both lessen. With this in mind, firms may spend money on capital goods in order to increase profitability, financing their expenditure through borrowing from the bank or using retained profit. In both cases, firms compare the investment project's estimated return rate with current interest rates. Figure-1 indicates a likely increase in level of investment (I_1-to-I_2), following the decrease in interest rates (0.75% to 0.1%), since there is simultaneously greater borrowing incentive, due to lower costs, and lesser saving incentive, given the lower reward.

Figure 1: The inverse relationship between interest rate and investment

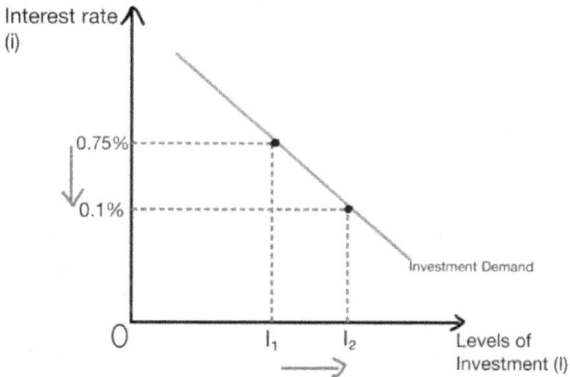

This expected increase in investment, a component of AD, thus leads to its increase, shifting the curve from AD_1-to-AD_2 (Figure-2), causing greater real output within the economy at Y_2 and an increase in average price level to PL_2. In this way, the BoE's **intervention** through lowering interest rates is intended to stimulate economic growth and recovery from the *"economic shock"* of Covid-19.

Moreover, the base rate reduction likely causes an increase in consumption, due to the *"lower[ed]...cost of borrowing"* and lessened reward for saving, intending to incentivise English consumers to borrow more money to purchase 'big-ticket' items, such as cars or houses, instead of depositing and saving. With saving disincentivised, consumption (another AD component) increases, shifting the curve right from AD_1-to-AD_2, as highlighted in Figure-2. Given consumption comprises roughly 70% of total UK AD, its increase, because of **intervention** through decreased interest rates, would significantly instigate economic growth, due to increased output at the new level Y_2, thus providing the fundamentals to economic recovery from a pandemic.

Figure 2: The effect of expansionary monetary policy on the UK macroeconomy

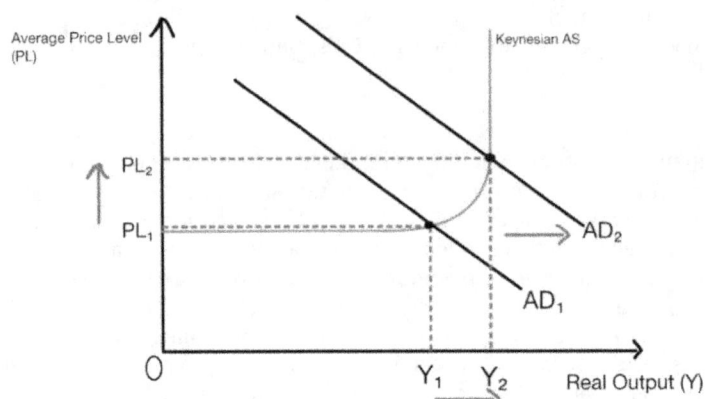

Despite this, the base rate reduction to 0.1% may not cause higher economic activity by increasing investments or consumption. The BoE cannot force firms' investment and consumers' expenditure, only incentivise them; business confidence is low at the moment, so a decision may be made to continue saving and not spend newfound liquidity, limiting any AD impact and thus economic growth. Additionally, expansionary monetary policy faces a time-lag of about 12-18 months before any noticeable impacts, by which many economic factors, crucial to the policy's success, may have changed.

Figure-2 also represents the theoretical effect of QE on UK AD, through the Bank's plan to *"increase...holdings of UK government and corporate bonds by £200bn"*. The purchase aims to increase the money supply within the economy by exchanging government-issued bonds for currency, then distributed to commercial banks. As these banks have more money to lend, they decrease interest rates to remain competitive, hence the two expansionary monetary policies of decreasing interest rates and QE are interlinked. Because of the injected money supply and complementary decreasing interest rates, investment and consumption increase, directly impacting AD with a right shift from AD_1-to-AD_2 (Figure-2), causing greater real output within the economy at Y_2, promoting economic growth and paving the route of recovery.

However, it may be argued that QE should be combined with fiscal policy for maximum efficacy, by maintaining spending and investment in the economy. If the QE drives yields down and banks are not using the created money, there is a necessity for the government to **intervene** through stimulating demand. This supports the BoE's belief that *"the measures...taken so far were not going to be enough and...a further package of measures [is] warranted"*, highlighting the requirement for supplemental policies to bolster the recovery approach for the UK economy.

Ultimately, assuming AD is the main driving force behind economic activity and there is significant spare capacity within the UK economy, **intervention** through a decreased base rate to 0.1% and QE worth £200bn, should lead to economic growth and *"help [the UK] cope with the economic damage caused by the virus"*. However, economic theory does not always translate in reality; these policies may fail, given their inability to force increases in components of AD, the time-lag involved in their implementation, and a potential lack of supporting fiscal stimuli. On balance, **intervention** of some form is imperative and the BoE ought *"to be on the offensive [and not]...wait [as recovery]...will be too late by then"*.

Commentary 2 cover sheet

Title of the article:	Experts urge minimum alcohol pricing in England after survey shows success
Source of the article:	The Guardian
Date article was published:	29 May 2021
URL of the article:	https://www.theguardian.com/society/2021/may/29/experts-urge-minimum-alcohol-pricing-in-england-after-survey-shows-success
Date article was accessed:	9 June 2021
Date commentary was written:	12 June 2021
Word count of the commentary:	796
Unit of the syllabus to which the article relates:	Unit 2: Microeconomics
Key concept being used:	Choice

Policy in Scotland and Wales has reduced consumption in heaviest drinking households

Image
Joanne Good, whose daughter Megan died in her sleep aged 16 after drinking strong white cider at a party. Photograph: Balance/PA

Campaigners have called for a minimum unit price (MUP) for alcohol in England after research showed it has reduced consumption in some of the heaviest drinking households in Scotland and Wales.

A 50p per unit price was introduced in Scotland in 2018 and an in-depth shopping survey two years on has found the policy has had a lasting impact.

A similar minimum unit price in Wales, brought in around the start of lockdown last year, has also brought positive change, the survey of 35,000 British households found.

Research by Newcastle University, published in the Lancet Public Health, showed the greatest reductions overall were in the purchase of ciders and spirits.

The impact was mainly seen in homes that bought the most alcohol – with the exception of high-purchasing households with the very lowest incomes, who did not change their habits despite the increase.

The research came amid fears about increased alcohol consumption across the UK during lockdown.

Prof Sir Ian Gilmore, the chair of the Alcohol Health Alliance, said: "Westminster has said time and time again that it is waiting for evidence from Scotland and Wales on minimum unit pricing – meanwhile, 80 people a day are dying from an alcohol-related cause.

"The evidence is here – it's time for the government to introduce minimum unit pricing in England in order to save lives, cut crime and reduce pressure on our NHS and emergency services."

Joanne Good, whose daughter Megan died in her sleep aged 16 after drinking strong white cider at a party, said: "Alcohol is too cheap and far too often ends up in the hands of children.

"I fully support any measure that increases the price of cheap alcohol and helps the young and vulnerable.

"I know the impact cheap, strong alcohol can have on people's lives, because it has devastated ours."

Prof Peter Anderson, from Newcastle University, who led the study, said: "Our previous work suggested that the introduction of an MUP in Scotland during May 2018 was associated with an immediate reduction in the amount of alcohol that households bought from shops or supermarkets.

"This latest analysis shows that the policy has continued to make an impact, with data showing a sustained drop in overall units of alcohol bought by some of the highest-consuming households, two years on.

"We can now see that the introduction of an MUP in Wales at the beginning of March 2020 has had a similar impact to the one we saw in Scotland in 2018.

"It will be interesting to see if this impact is sustained in Wales in the medium term, as it has been in Scotland."

Alison Douglas, the chief executive of Alcohol Focus Scotland, said the MUP should increase to 65p, adding: "This is hugely encouraging research from Newcastle University.

"Not only is MUP continuing to have the intended effect in reducing overall alcohol consumption in Scotland, it is those that tended to buy the most alcohol who are most likely to reduce the amount they purchase."

A government spokesperson said: "There are no plans to introduce minimum unit price in England at this time.

"We are committed to systematically addressing the causes of preventable deaths and ill-health, including the harmful consumption of alcohol, and this year we have outlined details of the new Office for Health Promotion which will spearhead these efforts."

This article discusses campaigners' efforts for *"minimum-unit pric[ing] (MUP) for alcohol in England"*, given prior success in Scotland and Wales. MUP is a form of government intervention through price controls, where minimum product prices (set by government/controlling authorities) are unable to adjust to their lower equilibrium level, determined by the free-market forces: demand and supply. Such intervention is necessary as the free market does not always lead to allocatively efficient outcomes for society in general. In England, since the unit-price of alcohol is low, the quantity demanded is high (according to the law of demand), which leads to socially detrimental overconsumption, given associated adverse health effects, like hepatitis. MUP implemented in England could lessen the *"harmful consumption of alcohol"* and promote better consumption **choices**; thus, this commentary's key concept is **choice**.

It is important for consumers to make better **choices** due to the negative consumption externalities which stem from *"heav[y] drinking"*. Figure-1 represents the market failure resulting from the existence of these externalities.

Figure 1: English alcohol market failure caused by negative consumption externality

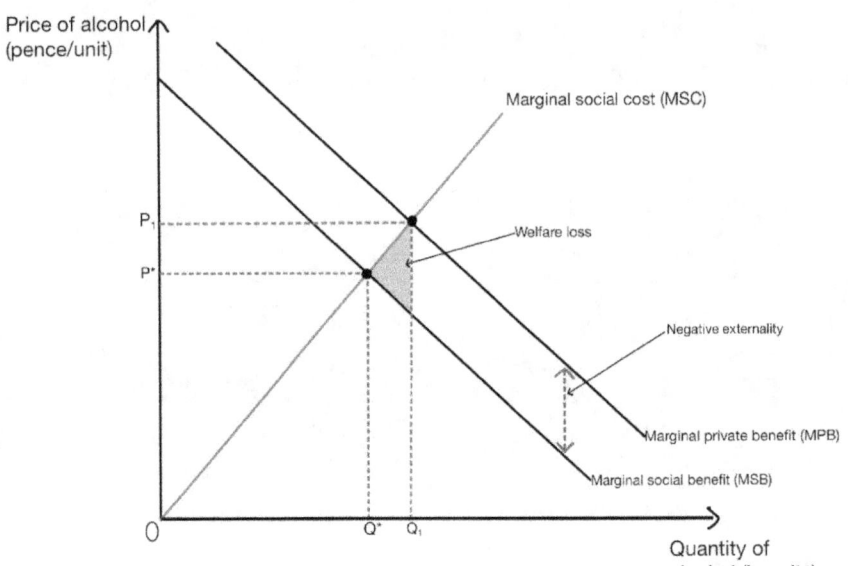

Market failure results since alcohol consumption leads to a divergence between *MSB* and *MPB*, caused by negative externalities including *"crime and...pressure on emergency services"*. These are suffered by third parties, thus presenting external costs, and diminishing *MSB*. Those who choose to consume alcohol maximise their *MPB*, and as there is a free market, consume where *MSC=MPB*, ignoring the negative externalities created. Therefore, alcohol is overconsumed at Q_1 for price P_1 and the overconsumption is Q_1-Q^*, where Q^* is the socially optimum output. As *MSC* is greater than *MSB* for these units, there is a welfare-loss (shaded above) to society with too many resources allocated to the English alcohol market.

To address the overconsumption and overproduction of the demerit good, the English government must intervene. Figure-2 displays the theoretical impacts of implementing MUP in the English alcohol market, based off similar *"evidence from Scotland and Wales"*. Without intervention, the equilibrium quantity demanded and supplied would be *Qe* at price *Pe,* where total economic welfare is maximised, however, societal welfare is not, given vast alcoholism. Thus, MUP is imposed at *Pmin.*

Figure 2: English alcohol market with MUP

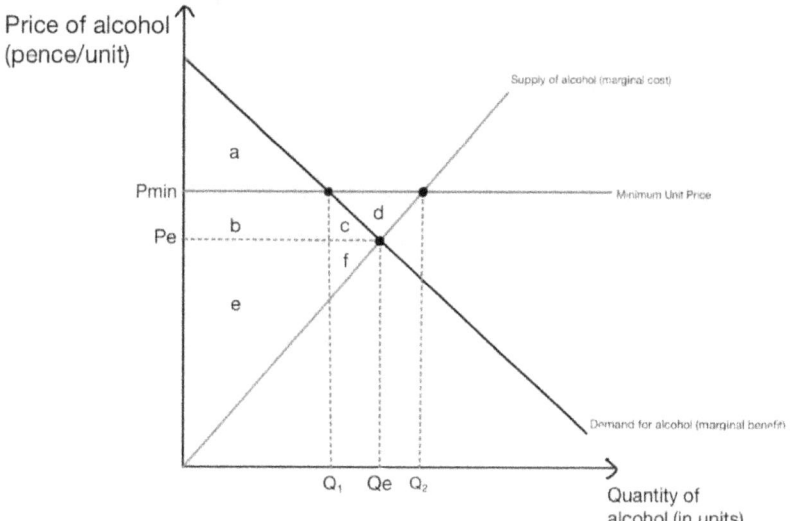

As the price rises from *Pe* to *Pmin,* quantity demanded falls from *Qe* to Q_1. As a result, consumer surplus decreases (from *a+b+c* to *a),* as they must now pay a higher price per unit for alcohol. The exact decrease in consumer demand for alcohol, is dependent upon the price elasticity of demand (PED). If similar results (to the Welsh and Scottish MUP) are observed, alcohol is most price-elastic for *"the highest-consuming households",* who demand less following MUP, since the good now accounts for a greater proportion of their disposable income. However, alcohol may also be considered price-inelastic, as it is addictive for some, who find it challenging to curtail their consumption. This was the case in Scotland for the *"high-purchasing households with the very lowest incomes" who* were an exception and *"did not change their habits"* despite MUP. Overall, consumers lose out when MUP is imposed, since they must either consume less of the product or now spend a greater proportion of their disposable income on it. Because of this, some may attempt to bypass MUP by sourcing their alcohol illegally; therefore, despite good intentions to *"address the causes of preventable deaths and ill-health",* MUP may also give rise to nefarious activity.

Whilst quantity demanded decreases to Q_1, quantity supplied increases from *Qe* to Q_2, since the price of alcohol increased, and firms seize the opportunity for greater profit margins. This causes a surplus of alcohol/excess supply *(d),* which may become problematic for producers if the government does not intervene further. Producers may be tempted to bypass MUP illegally, by selling at a price between *Pe* and *Pmin.* Overall, producer surplus likely increases (from *e+f to b+e*) as firms receive a higher product price and supply a larger quantity.

Firms' increase in revenue is determined by how price-elastic the alcohol is: more price-elastic alcohol, such as *"ciders and spirits... [which saw] the greatest [demand] reductions overall"* in Wales, will scarcely increase revenues, as compared with more price-inelastic alcohol, whose sustained demand contributes to larger revenues. Those firms enjoying an increase in revenue may be able to

121

increase employment opportunities, benefitting the labour market, which otherwise struggles with some workers too unwell to work, due to alcohol consumption.

Ultimately, if the English government *"introduce[s] minimum-unit pricing"*, Scottish and Welsh empirical evidence strongly suggests it would *"save lives, cut crime, and reduce pressure on...emergency services"*, as higher prices fulfil a rationing function, which benefits society by moderating alcoholism. However, MUP has drawbacks: its efficacy at rectifying the market failure is dependent on flexible price-elasticities and its implementation may lead to the rise of illicit activity. Therefore, the English government may consider alternative policies, such as indirect taxation or regulation, to help consumers make better **choices**.

Commentary 3 cover sheet

Title of the article:	Trump's Solar Tariffs Still Needed to Protect Industry, U.S. Agency Says
Source of the article:	Bloomberg
Date article was published:	24 November 2021
URL of the article:	https://www.bloomberg.com/news/articles/2021-11-24/u-s-says-trump-solar-tariffs-still-needed-to-protect-industry
Date article was accessed:	30 November 2021
Date commentary was written:	4 December 2021
Word count of the commentary:	798
Unit of the syllabus to which the article relates:	Unit 4: The global economy
Key concept being used:	Sustainability

Trump's Solar Tariffs Still Needed to Protect Industry, U.S. Agency Says

A U.S. trade agency has determined that tariffs on imported solar equipment, imposed by Donald Trump in 2018, are still necessary.

The U.S. International Trade Commission is expected to issue a recommendation by Dec. 8 on whether President Joe Biden should extend the duties, after voting unanimously Wednesday that imported solar products remain a threat to U.S. manufacturers.

The decision underscores the tensions between the administration's sometimes dueling goals. While the White House is focused on boosting clean energy production in the U.S., it is also keen to support domestic manufacturing -- and union jobs. Extending the tariffs would be a blow to U.S. solar installers that rely heavily on imported panels, but would aid those that manufacture components within the U.S.

Import relief "continues to be necessary to prevent or remedy serious injury to the U.S. industry, and that there is evidence that the domestic industry is making a positive adjustment to import competition," the ITC said in a statement.
Biden is expected to make a final decision before the four-year tariff is scheduled to expire in February and is under no obligation to abide by the ITC's recommendation.

First Solar Inc., the biggest U.S. panel maker, advanced as much as 3.4% Wednesday, while installer Sunrun Inc. slumped as much as 4.2% and the Chinese panel maker JinkoSolar Holding Co. fell 3.5%. In early trading in China on Thursday, JA Solar Technology Co. lost as much as 6.6%, Trina Solar Co. slipped 4.6% and Longi Green Energy Technology Co. dropped as much as 3%.
Despite a slight uptick in U.S. solar panel-making since the start of the Trump presidency, China remains the world's predominant solar manufacturer. The U.S. depends on products made in Thailand, Malaysia and Vietnam for most new capacity. Tariff proponents have asserted that the duties are needed to help U.S. manufacturers compete with cheap panels -- especially those made by Chinese companies -- thus creating domestic jobs and bolstering America's energy security.

"Four years of tariffs has proven to be an ineffective way to incentivize solar manufacturing and create American jobs," Abigail Ross Hopper, chief executive officer of the trade group Solar Energy Industries Association, said in an emailed statement. "A new round of Trump-imposed safeguard tariffs will hamper U.S. solar development in their wake, and we hope President Biden sees the damage they will cause to his clean energy vision."

When Biden first took office, an extension of Trump's tariffs was seen as unlikely by many in the solar industry. Some in the sector even speculated that he would move to eliminate them. But that hope quickly passed.

While the Biden administration has made boosting clean energy a key goal, it's also tangled with China on solar.

The U.S. in June barred imports of some solar products made in China's Xinjiang region in an effort to counter alleged human-rights abuses against that country's ethnic Uyghur Muslim minority. Xinjiang makes about half the world's polysilicon, a key ingredient in most solar panels.

This article discusses President Biden's upcoming decision on whether Donald Trump's *"[expiring] four-year tariff"* on imported solar equipment is *"still necessary"*, as one US trade agency has determined. These tariffs are specific taxes, issued by US government, on solar equipment imported into the US; they aim to *"protect the [domestic solar] industry"* by increasing foreign firms' production costs and subsequently, product prices, which helps US solar equipment manufacturers to compete on price. With Biden *"focussed on boosting clean energy production in the US"*, an increase in US solar development would certainly help the economy transition to one more environment-friendly; thus, this commentary's key concept is **sustainability**.

Any specific tax placed upon a good shifts the supply curve upwards by the amount of the tax. Likewise, the current US solar tariff shifts the world supply curve for solar equipment upwards, as it affects only foreign producers. This is shown in Figure-1, displaying the current US solar equipment market, with tariff, and the intended outcome *"should [Biden] extend the duties"*.

Figure 1: The impact of the current solar equipment tariff (US perspective)

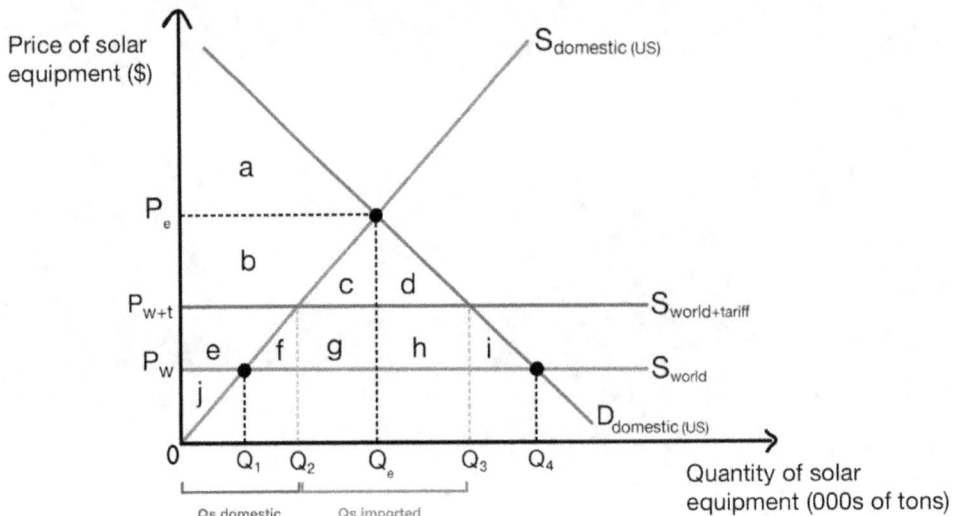

Figure-1 assumes two properties. Firstly, foreign solar equipment producers are willing and able to supply any quantity at the world price, thus under free trade world supply is perfectly price-elastic at *Pw*, and *Pw+t* after tariff imposition. Secondly, foreign producers, like *"Chinese panel maker JinkoSolar Holding Co"* have comparative advantage in solar equipment production, meaning their opportunity cost of supplying solar goods to the US is lower than domestic producers'. Therefore, *Pw* is lower than the domestic equilibrium price, *Pe*.

In free trade domestic solar manufacturers were only willing to supply *Q₁* at price *Pw;* their producer surplus was area *j. "US solar installers...rely[ing]...on imported panels"* however, demanded *Q₄* units for price *Pw*, thus excess domestic demand existed *(Q₄-Q₁),* which foreign producers provided. Such domestic purchases of foreign solar equipment are *"a threat to US manufacturers' [employment]"* as resulting losses in both revenue and demand for labour weaken the domestic industry. By choosing to extend the current tariff, Biden would help US manufacturers compete on price, inducing *"import relief...to support domestic manufacturing and union jobs"*.

With tariff, domestic manufacturers are incentivised to increase output, from Q_1 to Q_2, due to the higher price, $Pw+t$. Consequently, producer surplus increased since free trade *(area j to j+e)* and their revenues too. The extent to which they have and may continue to benefit depends on the price-elasticity of demand for solar equipment and the tariff's magnitude. The US International Trade Commission supports this protectionist success, stating *"the domestic industry is making a positive adjustment to import competition"*.

Though tariff-extension supports US solar manufacturers, it *"would be a blow to US solar installers"*: the primary consumers of solar equipment. They resume paying the higher price, Pw, but now for fewer goods *(Q_4-Q_3)*, due to a decrease in 'real' income, incentivising consumption of substitute solar equipment with greater satisfaction-price ratio. In the long-run an extended tariff may also deter foreign producers from trading in the US, reducing solar-product variety for US solar installers. If Biden therefore discontinues protectionism, agreeing *"a new round of...tariffs will hamper US solar development"*, consumer surplus could increase from area *a+b+c+d* with tariff, to free trade value, *a+b+c+d+e+f+g+h+i*. This demonstrates a trade-off: helping US manufacturers compete by maintaining tariff protection versus incentivising clean energy installation and economic **sustainability** through free trade with China: *"the world's predominant solar manufacturer"*.

For the US government, solar tariff renewal would continually provide tax revenue (equal to area *g+h*), which may help finance Biden's *"key goal...of boosting clean energy"* to increase economic **sustainability**. Alternatively, it could cover costs associated with tariff enforcement and administration. If Biden does not *"extend the tariffs"*, he must consider the lost tax revenue and possible cost of unemployment benefits, to support domestic citizens who lose employment in the solar industry, due to *"import competition"* regaining cost advantages in solar equipment production.

"Eliminat[ing] the tariffs" would improve market efficiency, by regaining the two deadweight-losses in welfare, equal to areas *f+i*. 'f' is associated with inefficient production, where excessive resources are used by the less efficient and less **sustainable** US solar manufacturers to produce Q_2 solar equipment. 'i' represents the loss to solar installers, who pay a higher price for fewer goods. Overall welfare would also increase, highlighted by the community surplus increase: *a+b+c+d+e+g+h+j* (with tariff) to *a+b+c+d+e+f+g+h+i+j* (without).

Ultimately, in deciding whether to extend solar tariffs, Biden must determine his priority objective for the solar industry: increase economic **sustainability** by *"boosting clean energy production...[or]...support domestic manufacturing"*, as these *"duelling goals"* unlikely occur mutually. A tariffed market supports domestic solar manufacturers, but forfeits market efficiency, overall welfare, and the variety of solar equipment for domestic installers. If Biden decides *"prevent[ing]...injury to US solar manufacturing"* with tariffs is more beneficial, he must consider retaliation through reciprocal protectionist policies, particularly as it *"tangles with China"*.

5. PORTFOLIO FIVE

Author: Thomas Beck
Moderated Mark: 43/45
Level: Economics HL

Economics Commentary 1

Title of Article: Tax changes planned for cigarettes and alcohol in South Africa - but they could come at a cost

Source of article: BusinessTech <https://tinyurl.com/5xk8fkum> [Accessed 28/07/21]

Date article was published: 29/06/21

Date commentary was written: 28/07/21

Word count of the commentary: 800

Unit of syllabus to which the article relates: Microeconomics

Key concept being used: Economic well-being

1   Article

Tax changes planned for cigarettes and alcohol in South Africa - but they could come at a cost

Staff Writer — 29 June 2021

In its February 2021 budget, the National Treasury announced an 8% increase in alcohol and tobacco excise duties. This excise increase appeared to be driven by a desire to grow government revenue, after a year in which the economy - and government coffers - were battered from the Covid-19 crisis, says Virusha Subban, partner and head of Indirect Tax at Baker McKenzie Johannesburg. At the same time, Treasury announced plans to amend its excise policy on cigarettes and alcohol. "In particular, Treasury noted it was considering levying higher excise duties on cigarettes and alcohol in future," Subban said. "In his budget statement, the minister of finance Tito Mboweni said that the government would review so-called 'sin taxes' as part of the country's public health agenda, to reduce consumption through higher retail prices." Current excise policy limits the excise to 40% of the retail price of the most popular price category of cigarettes. The targeted excise incidence for spirits is 36%, for beer it is 23% and for wine it's 11%.

Taxed to the hilt

Over the past couple of years, Treasury has been setting excise outside the prescribed boundaries of its own excise policy, Subban said. "For example, prior to the February Budget, cigarette excise was at 43.5% of the retail price, which is apparently ultra vires to the Government's own excise policy. "The 8% excise increase took the incidence on the most popular category of cigarettes to 45%." The responsibility of advising on tax policy and designing new tax legislation rests on the finance minister, working closely with Treasury. But there needs to be a proper consultation process where the voice of businesses and their customers are invited to heard, Subban said. The Constitutional Court and the Supreme Court of Appeal both say that policymakers have a Constitutional obligation to facilitate public participation in the taxation law and policymaking process. Consultation with alcohol and tobacco manufacturers at an early stage of the pending excise tax policy review is imperative, Subban said. "But, as things stand, no announcements have been made about how the consultation process will run, what it will entail and how long it will take. "Given the country's Constitutional obligations and its aim to build a better fiscal policy technical capacity, it is important that Treasury lays out clear and transparent plans for consultation on the excise policy as soon as possible, so that all interested parties can make a proper contribution." This is especially important given recent developments in the legal alcohol and tobacco industries, she said.

Tread carefully

The alcohol and tobacco industries were both severely impacted by government policy during the pandemic. During the 2020 national lockdown, the government imposed an unprecedented total trading ban on alcohol from the end of March to the beginning of June, with further restrictions in place for the rest of 2020. Cigarette sales were banned between March and August. This resulted in a drastic drop in legal sales of these products, a corresponding fall in tax revenues, and a rapid rise in the consumption of tax-evading, illicit, alternatives. According to the University of Cape Town, the illicit cigarette market grew by 104% during the lockdown period. And a recent IPSOS study shows that over 60% of the cigarettes consumed in South Africa are now illicit, up by 33% compared to before the sales ban. Consequently, in the 2020/21 financial year, excise duties from legal cigarettes were a staggering 60% lower than the R14.46 billion the Treasury expected to collect. The alcohol industry also reported large losses. The South African Liquor Brand Owners Association said that the sales bans cost the legal alcohol industry R36 billion in lost revenues and the Treasury, R29 billion in lost tax receipts. They also estimate that 15% of the alcohol market has continued to operate illegally, without paying any taxes. "There are signs that the supply chain for illicit products have gained substantial ground, with more sophisticated distribution models having been formed during the sales bans. Even after sales restrictions were lifted, the consumption of tax-evading alcohol and tobacco products was higher than they were pre-Covid," Subban said. It further cautioned that the changes to taxes could come at other costs - including pushing businesses out of the country. "We should not forget the contributions made to the history of this country by these industries, from job creation through to fiscal contributions and innovation in their respective spaces. "Let us not give multinational companies a reason to exit a country where illegal business practices are becoming the norm."

2 Commentary

The article discusses plans by the South African Treasury to impose "higher excise duties on cigarettes" using an ad valorem tax (a tax based of a percentage of the price) in light of the "country's public health agenda", which aims to improve the **economic wellbeing** (a concept which encompasses factors including income security and living a satisfactory quality of life) of its citizens through the reduced consumption of cigarettes.

The market for cigarettes creates negative consumption externalities (external costs to a third party arising from excess consumption) from the spill-over costs of consuming cigarettes (e.g. the increased burden placed on health care services) which consumers do not account for when choosing to consume cigarettes.

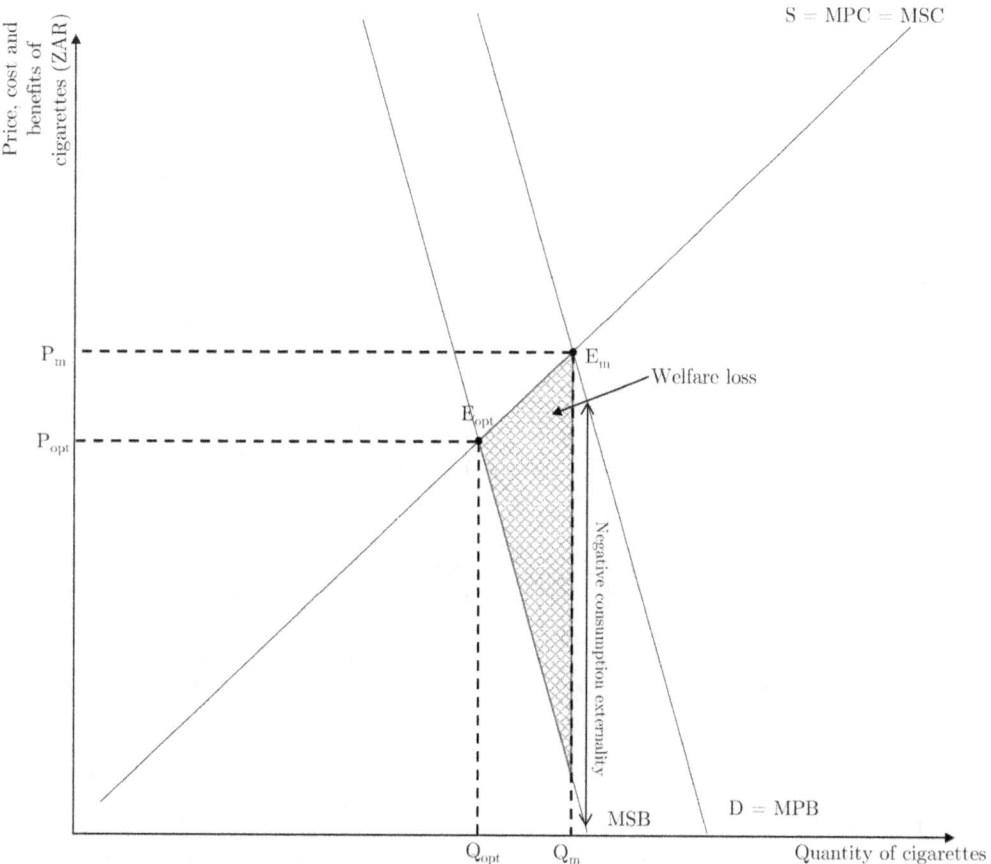

Figure 1: Externalities in the South African cigarette market

The free market produces at the equilibrium E_m, where the marginal private benefit of consuming cigarettes (MPB) is equal to the marginal private cost to manufactures of producing cigarettes (MPC) at quantity Q_m and price P_m. However, because of the external costs that society faces from consuming cigarettes, the benefit to society of consuming one additional cigarette (MSB) is lower than the MPB received. For society overall, it is more beneficial to produce where the MSB equals the marginal social cost of producing cigarettes (MSC). This is at the equilibrium E_{opt} with a quantity Q_{opt} and price P_{opt}. Therefore, since $Q_m > Q_{opt}$, the free market overconsumes cigarettes resulting in a welfare loss (shaded) which may reduce the **economic wellbeing** of South African citizens.

In response, the South African Treasury has already imposed "sin taxes" on cigarettes with a "cigarette excise at 43.5%" and plans an "8% excise increase ... to 45%".

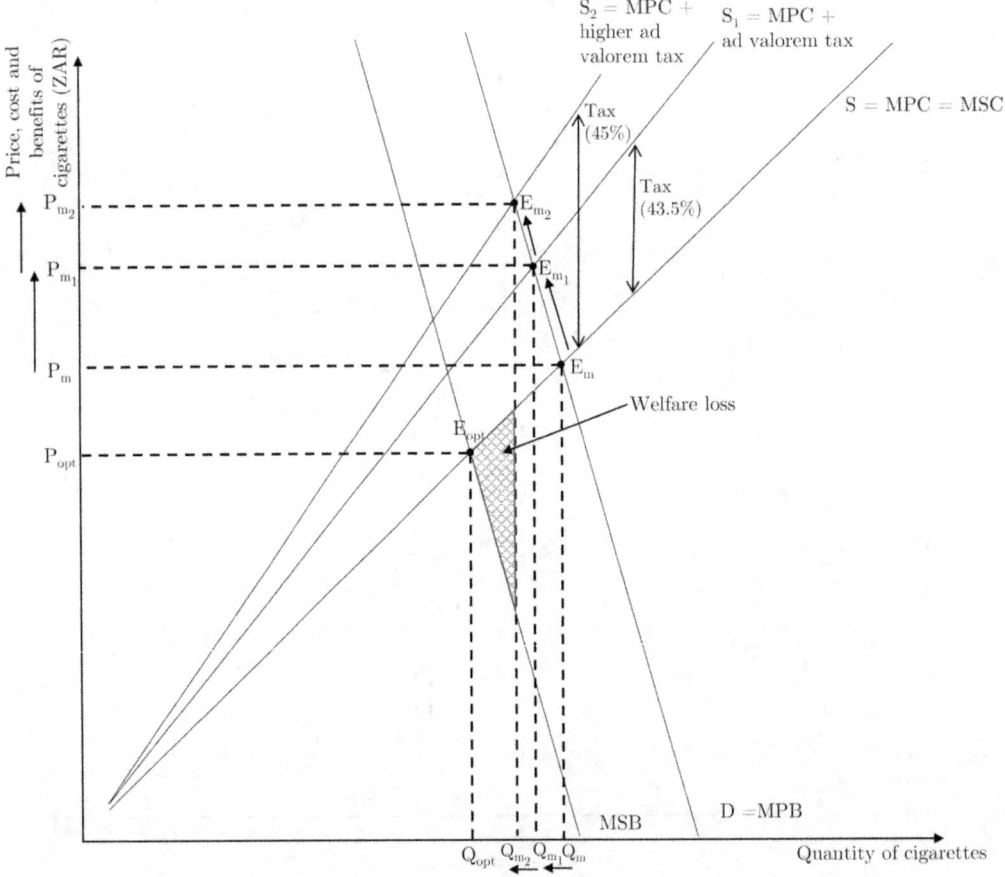

Figure 2: Increased taxation in the South African cigarette market

134

The cigarette market already has an ad valorem tax implemented at a incidence of 43.5% which causes an inward shift of supply from S to S_1 as the costs to cigarette producers rise (hence why MPC rises). This establishes a new market equilibrium at E_{m_1} and economic theory suggests this reduces the cigarette quantity from Q_m to Q_{m_1} and increases the price of cigarettes from P_m to P_{m_1}. If the Treasury then increases the incidence rate to 45%, it shifts supply further inwards from S_1 to S_2 and by the same logic forms a new equilibrium at E_{m_2}. This is at an increased cigarette market price of P_{m_2} and a lesser cigarette quantity of Q_{m_2}. Since the quantity of cigarettes consumed has decreased towards the optimum quantity (Q_{opt}), the welfare loss has also decreased as indicated by the smaller triangle and so the **economic wellbeing** of citizens should theoretically increase.

This policy should help recuperate the "R29 billion lost in tax" as the government sees increased tax revenue. Any revenue gained could be used to fund government spending which may cause further increases in **economic wellbeing** but it must be spent with the purpose of improving **economic wellbeing**. However, previous actions by the government including banning the sale of cigarettes has led the illicit cigarette market to grow by 104% which reduces the effectiveness of such government policy as illicit markets would not contribute towards tax revenues. Additionally, its size is likely to grow given the planned increases in tax rates which pushes consumers who are no longer willing and/ or able to pay the rising prices into the illicit markets.

The ban of cigarette sales likely also caused massive losses for cigarette firms and so such increases in taxation (which reduce revenues further) may mean some firms shut down or even move abroad. This would mean that their domestic workers are now unemployed and suffer loss of incomes leading to decreases in **economic wellbeing** for them but in the long run, they can likely find employment in other industries.

Furthermore, the plan to "reduce consumption through higher retail prices" may also be ineffective since the demand for cigarettes tends to be price inelastic meaning consumers are not very responsive to changes in price since cigarettes are addicting. This is shown in Figure 2 by the price inelastic MPB curve and this also shows that the level of taxation needed to achieve Q_{opt} would be so high that it is virtually impossible given the countries poor "fiscal policy technical capacity" as well as it likely causing further growth in the illicit cigarette market. However, in the long run, demand for cigarettes does tend to be more price-sensitive as persistently higher prices may motivate people to stop smoking and so higher taxation may be effective in the long term.

In conclusion, whilst the plan to increase taxation on cigarettes should aid the government in reducing cigarette consumption, thereby improving the **economic wellbeing** of its citizens, the previous actions of the government bring this into question. The effectiveness of this policy in achieving those goals will likely depend on whether the government can act effectively to decrease the size of the growing illicit cigarette market.

Economics Commentary 2

Title of Article: Japan approves a \$490 billion economic stimulus package as the pandemic's effects linger

Source of article: The New York Times <https://www.nytimes.com/2021/11/19/world/asia/japan-stimulus.html> [Accessed 14/02/22]

Date article was published: 19/11/21

Date commentary was written: 14/02/22

Word count of the commentary: 799

Unit of syllabus to which the article relates: Macroeconomics

Key concept being used: Intervention

1 Article

Japan approves a $490 billion economic stimulus package as the pandemic's effects linger

Hikari Hida — Nov. 19, 2021

Japan's government agreed on Friday to spend $490 billion on stimulus measures, a move by its prime minister to boost an economy battered by coronavirus restrictions and by a supply chain crunch that has affected the country's largest manufacturers.

Japan announced a partial easing of border restrictions this month and has lifted virtually all restrictions on its economy amid a falling virus caseload. And its rate of fully vaccinated people — 76 percent of the population, according to a New York Times tracker — is one of the highest among rich nations. But a ban on international tourists continues to weigh on economic growth.

The stimulus package, Japan's largest to date, accounts for about 10 percent of the country's economic output, officials said. Prime Minister Fumio Kishida said on Friday that it could increase economic output about 5.6 percent.

"I want to bring Japan's economy, which has been severely damaged, onto a trajectory of recovery," he told reporters.

The package includes aid to struggling businesses and hospitals, money for strengthening semiconductor supply chains, and programs to encourage domestic tourism and investment in a nationwide university endowment fund.

It also includes a one-time cash handout of 100,000 yen, or $878, per child under 18 for households where the highest-earning parent is paid less than about $84,300 a year. About nine in 10 households with children are eligible.

The cash handouts to young families are not especially popular. Critics have questioned the need for them in a country with an aging society.

Last spring, the government sent stimulus checks to every resident, but they did little to raise inflation or consumer spending. Analysts estimate that about 70 percent of the handouts went to household savings.

Mr. Kishida's cabinet approved the stimulus package on Friday, less than two months after he won a runoff election for leadership of the country's governing Liberal Democratic Party. Japan's economy is the world's third largest after those of the United States and China.

2 Commentary

The article discusses an **intervention** (when governments act to try and 'correct' the free market) by the Japanese government to stimulate economic growth in the country after the pandemic by using expansionary fiscal policy (increased government spending and/ or decreased taxation to increase the level of economic activity). Whilst this **intervention** would theoretically boost economic growth, the policies employed leave doubts about the effectiveness of this **intervention**.

In Japan, a "supply chain crunch" due to a shortage of semiconductors has caused rising business costs for largest manufacturers in Japan meaning the short-run aggregate supply (SRAS) curve shifts inwards from SRAS to $SRAS_1$. Simultaneously, "coronavirus restrictions" imposed are likely to reduce domestic consumption as well as investment due to increased pessimism about the future. Since both of these are components of aggregate demand (AD), AD would also shift inwards from AD to AD_1.

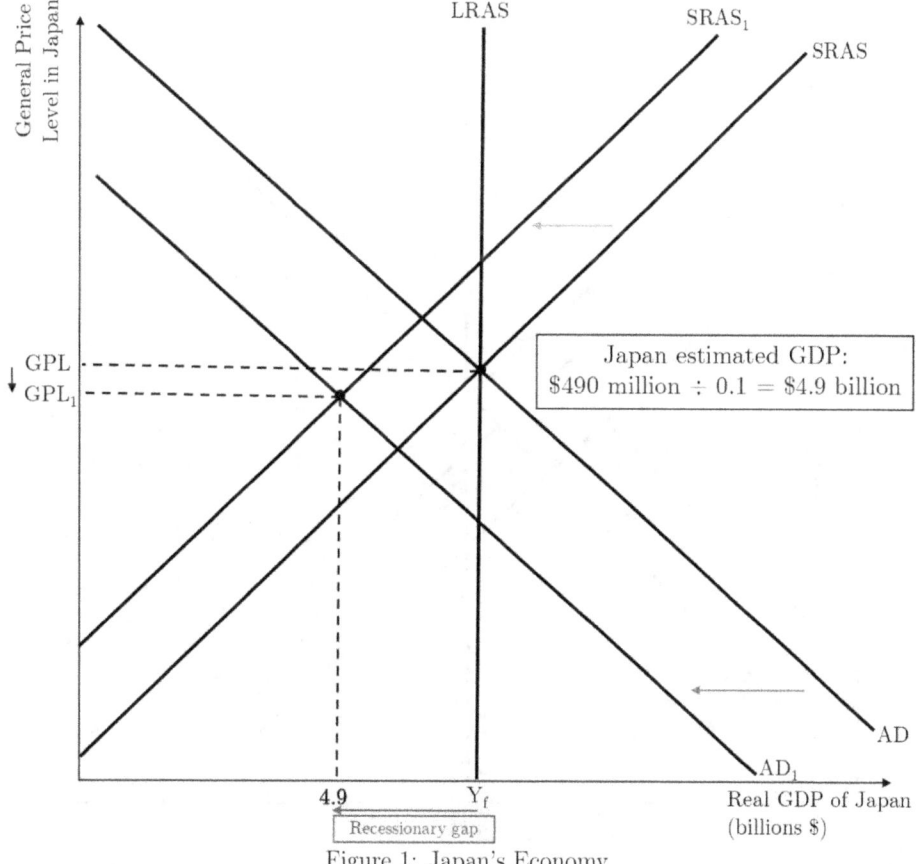

Figure 1: Japan's Economy

139

This likely puts a downward pressure of general prices from GPL to GPL_1 and has reduced GDP to $4.9 billion, below the full-employment level of output of Y_f; hence, creating a recessionary gap.

The $490 million stimulus **intervention** should bring the economy onto "a trajectory of recovery" as economic theory predicts that it should cause a significant initial increase in AD (AD_1 to AD_2) since consumption and investment are the main components of AD in a developed economy like Japan and rising disposable incomes through the cash handouts and greater domestic tourism should lead to greater consumption overall as well as increased investment due to the new endowment fund. Furthermore, due to this extensive government spending, the multiplier effect also plays a part as through individuals and firms receiving greater income, other stakeholders gain rising incomes and so, theoretically, this causes induced spending through increases in their consumption/ investment leading to further outward shifts of AD (AD_2 to AD). Additionally, the "strengthening of semiconductor supply chains" likely reduces business costs as semiconductors are a key manufacturing component and so this causes an outward shift in SRAS ($SRAS_1$ to SRAS).

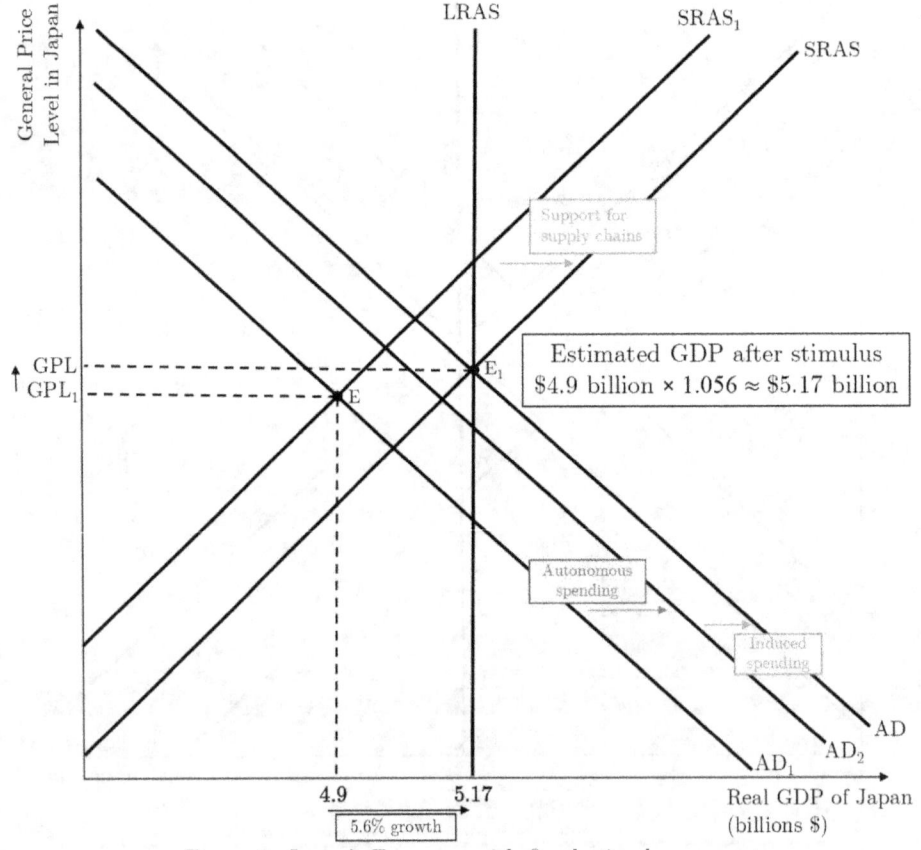

Figure 2: Japan's Economy with fiscal stimulus support

Assuming the full employment level of output to be \$5.17 billion (the government predicted increase in GDP), this policy should help close the recessionary gap as a new equilibrium is formed at E_1 and place some upward price pressure from GPL_1 to GPL. This economic growth should also reduce unemployment through firms hiring more workers to produce more output and the upward price pressure is likely even desirable considering Japan's history with deflation.

However, this **intervention** by the government may not be as effective as predicted, since not only do the cash handouts only apply parents of younger children (which does not impact many consumers in an "aging society") but additionally, additional income received by most consumers after the last stimulus was predominantly saved with a high marginal propensity to save of 0.7. This means that the initial outward shift in AD is reduced due to lower additional spending and by this logic, the size of induced spending and the subsequent multiplier effect is also dramatically reduced; limiting the possible AD impact.

The **intervention** of the government in "semiconductor supply chains" may not be able to re-solve all the bottlenecks that are occurring and it will ultimately be accompanied by a significant time lag as these issues cannot be fixed easily due to their complexity. However, it is likely a neces-sary government **intervention** due to the reliance of so many firms including the "country's largest manafacturers" on semiconductors and so, by at least rectifying some of the issues, the overall supply side impact should be reduced.

Despite this, there could still be more appropriate/ effective forms of **intervention** for the demand side impact as currently a big obstacle to economic growth is the "ban on international tourits". Despite efforts by the government to "encourage domestic tourism", it will likely be ineffective at restoring the same level of consumption that international tourists would and may be hampered further by low domestic confidence. However, the reduction of international tourists should reduce the demand for the Japanese Yen though which would cause the currency to depreciate which could, in fact, make exports more competitive abroad. However, again, the loss in growth through the lack of international tourists likely outweighs the minimal gains from increased exports due to a weaker currency and additionally, fewer international tourists are unlikely to have a significant impact on the exchange rate.

In conclusion, despite the **intervention** by the Japanese government likely being necessary in light of stagnating economic growth, the exact strategy employed may be ineffective in the short run due to the issues discussed above. Even in the long run, the specific **intervention** employed may only be able to solve part of the supply side issues and not the demand deficient aspects but likely the pandemic's impact on demand will have significantly reduced by then.

Economics Commentary 3

Title of Article: Bourbon distillers face big tax bills and higher tariffs after a record year for production

Source of article: CNBC <https://tinyurl.com/4b4t87c3> [Accessed 27/11/21]

Date article was published: 06/10/21

Date commentary was written: 27/11/21

Word count of the commentary: 796

Unit of syllabus to which the article relates: The Global Economy

Key concept being used: Equity

1 Article

Bourbon distillers face big tax bills and higher tariffs after a record year for production

Amanda Macias — Wed, Oct 6 2021

WASHINGTON – For the first time there are more than 10 million barrels of bourbon aging across Kentucky, and distillers set records by filling nearly 2.5 million barrels in a single year.

That all sounds like a triumph for America's native whiskey. Yet bourbon producers are contending with trade fights that hurt sales and a pandemic that is hampering tourism. Bigger tariffs are in store later this year.

There's also a hefty, one-of-a-kind tax bill due.

Distillers in Kentucky are slated to pay more than $33 million in aging barrel taxes in 2021 alone. That figure is 140% higher than it was 10 years ago.

"This is truly a historic and landmark record but that milestone comes with a cost," Eric Gregory, president of the Kentucky Distillers' Association, said about the record production and tax rates. Because bourbon-aging barrels are considered property, they are subject to property tax in Kentucky, Gregory said.

"Every year that barrel ages, it is taxed again and again and again and again," he said. "If you're drinking a bottle of 18-year-old Elijah Craig, that whiskey from that barrel had been taxed 18 times before it was bottled."

"No other place in the world does this, they don't do it in Japanese whiskey, or Canadian whiskey or Scotch whiskey or Irish whiskey or even Tennessee whiskey. We're the only place in the world that taxes aging barrels as spirits," Gregory said.

The tax puts Kentucky distillers at a competitive disadvantage, he added: "Not only does it raise prices, but that is important capital that we could be using to invest here in Kentucky."

In addition to the aging-barrel taxes, Kentucky distillers are set to pay approximately $300 million in state and local taxes and another $1.8 billion in federal excise taxes on alcohol.

Then there are the tariffs.

'Our industry is collateral damage'

Since the entirety of bourbon production can only occur within the U.S., per a 1964 congressional resolution that called it a "distinctive product of the United States," a tariff on the drink comes

144

across as a strategic political punch to Kentucky, which is represented by Sen. Mitch McConnell, the top Republican in the Senate.

Kentucky's unique climate and pure limestone water is why the Bluegrass State is considered the birthplace of bourbon, responsible for 95% of the world's supply. Kentucky's bourbon business employs approximately 20,100 workers and generates a smooth $8.6 billion annually.

"No other country in the world can produce a whiskey and call it bourbon. So when you're looking at something to target that is uniquely American and can't move its production overseas, bourbon is a good target," Gregory explained. "There are no winners in trade wars, only consequences and we're a consequence."

In 2018, China, Mexico, Canada the European Union and the United Kingdom imposed retaliatory tariffs on American whiskey in response to U.S. Section 232 tariffs on steel and aluminum.

Since the imposition of 25% tariffs on American whiskey, exports to the EU, the largest export market for the spirit, plunged 37% from $702 million in 2018 to $440 million in 2020, according to figures provided by the Distilled Spirits Council.

Bourbon exports to the UK, the fourth-largest market for American whiskey, declined by 53% from $150 million in 2018 to $71 million in 2020.

In 2019, a long-running trade battle between U.S. aerospace titan Boeing and European rival Airbus took an anxious turn when the Trump administration imposed a 25% retaliatory tariff on single malt Scotch whisky and single malt Irish whiskey from Northern Ireland, and certain liqueurs and cordials from Europe.

Tit-for-tat retaliatory tariffs across the Atlantic ensued, further exacerbating problems for the bourbon industry.

"The tariffs have been devastating," Gregory said. "Our industry is collateral damage in trade disputes that have nothing to do with bourbon."

Earlier this year, the Biden administration alongside the EU and UK agreed to suspend tariffs on distilled spirits and wine targeted in the Airbus and Boeing dispute for the next five years.

The 25% tariff on American whiskeys in the steel and aluminum dispute persists, though, making bourbon the only spirit subject to duties in an ongoing transatlantic trade row.

Double shot of trouble

Despite bars and restaurants closing down for stretches last year due to the Covid pandemic, sales in America's whiskey sector rose 8.2% year-over-year to 4.3 billion, according to data compiled by the Distilled Spirits Council of the United States.

Domestic volumes of bourbon, Tennessee whiskey and rye whiskey rose 7% to 28.4 million cases, an indication of strong demand across price ranges.

Yet the 25% percent tariffs triggered by steel and aluminum duties still loom large and are set to double on Dec. 1.

"The tariffs on American whiskey have left a path of destruction impacting both sides of the Atlantic, from U.S. distillers and farmers to EU and UK restaurants, bars and consumers" said Lisa Hawkins, senior vice president of public affairs for the Distilled Spirits Council of the United States.

"These tariffs continue to be a significant and unnecessary drag on the recovery of craft distilleries across the U.S. that had to close their tasting rooms and tours for months on end due to the pandemic," she said.

The nation's top trade chief said Monday that the Biden administration is working to resolve the outstanding steel and aluminum trade issue with Europe in order to stoke greater cooperation on challenges posed by China.

"The engagement with the EU follows the same line of thinking and spirit as the approach that we took to large civil aircraft. Which is, how do you take a situation of tension and work through it to convert it into a partnership and collaboration," U.S. Trade Representative Katherine Tai said when asked about dissolving the trade dispute.

"And that is certainly what we are working on and our goal in that exercise," Tai said, without providing further details.

Distillers are dreading the coming tariff hike.

"It'll be crippling. It will all but force some distillers out of the European market, it will be a crippling blow for bourbon and whiskey," Gregory said.

"We've lost over $200 million in exports at 25% and now double that," he said. "That's what we're looking at."

2 Commentary

The article discusses plans by the EU to increase tariffs (a tax on imports) on US Whiskey and Bourbon in retaliation against tariffs imposed by the US and discusses the impact on US producers which raises questions about the **equity** (the concept of fairness within a situation) of this decision.

The suitability of the US with its "unique climate" to produce bourbon and whiskey means it can produce "95% of the world's supply" (a far greater quantity than EU domestic producers (S_{EU}) hence, the perfectly elastic US supply curve of S_{US}) at a lower price, P_{US}, than the EU domestic price, P_{EU}.

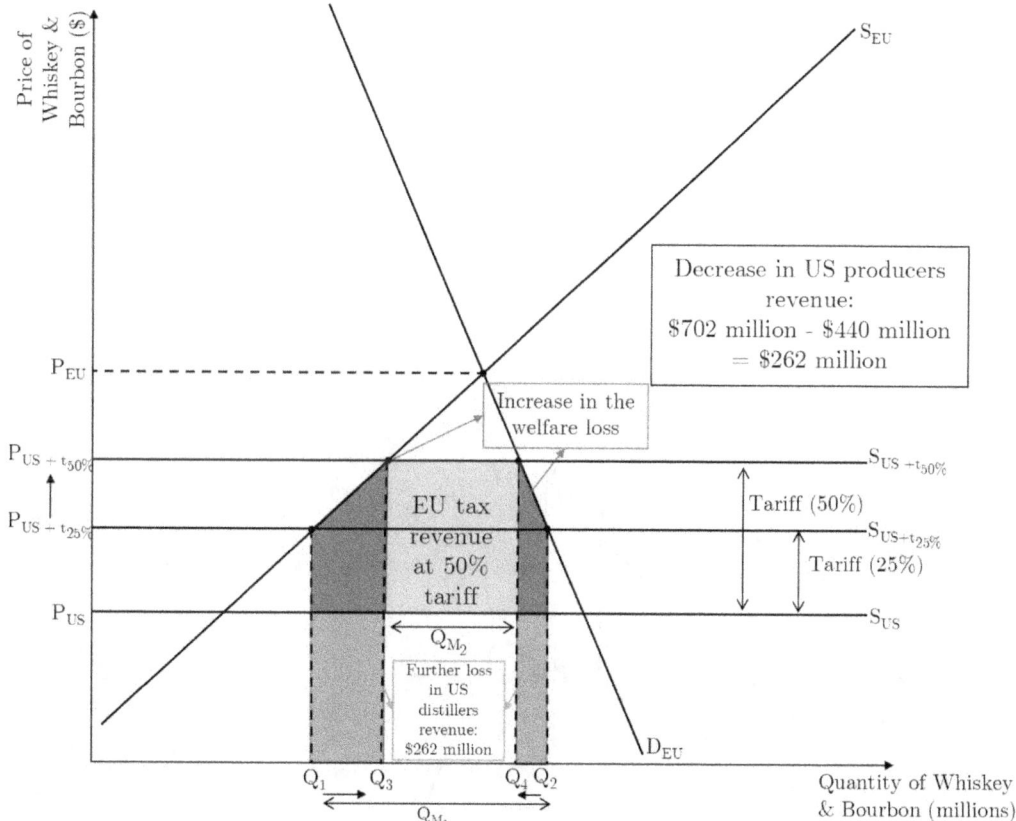

Figure 1: EU Whiskey and Bourbon Market with increased tariff

Initially, with the existing 25% tariff, domestic EU whiskey firms can produce a quantity of Q_1 at price $P_{US + t_{25\%}}$ but the demand exceeds the quantity supplied at Q_2. This shortage is then supplied by imports of whiskey which supply the quantity Q_{M_1} ($Q_2 - Q_1$). The increased tariff of 50% on whiskey imports then shifts the US supply curve inwards to $S_{US + t_{50\%}}$ at price $P_{US + t_{50\%}}$. At this increased price, domestic EU firms now produce an increased quantity of Q_3 and EU consumers now demand less whiskey at quantity Q_4 and so imports decrease to Q_{M_2}. Whilst, slightly less consumption of whiskey could be positive as it is a demerit good, the welfare loss increases from what it was previously as indicated due to the loss in consumer surplus. Additionally, the EU would gain tax revenue as given by the incidence of the tax multiplied by the quantity of imports as indicated which would increase from the level collected before as the demand for whiskey tends to be price inelastic due to the lack of close substitutes and its addictive nature; as indicated by the price elasticity of D_{EU}. Furthermore, if the overall revenue loss is now "double that", US distillers stand to lose another $262 million due to lower levels of exportation.

This policy may, unintentionally, be **inequitable** as US producers may suffer disproportionately when considering that they are already taxed at a rate that "no other place in the world does".

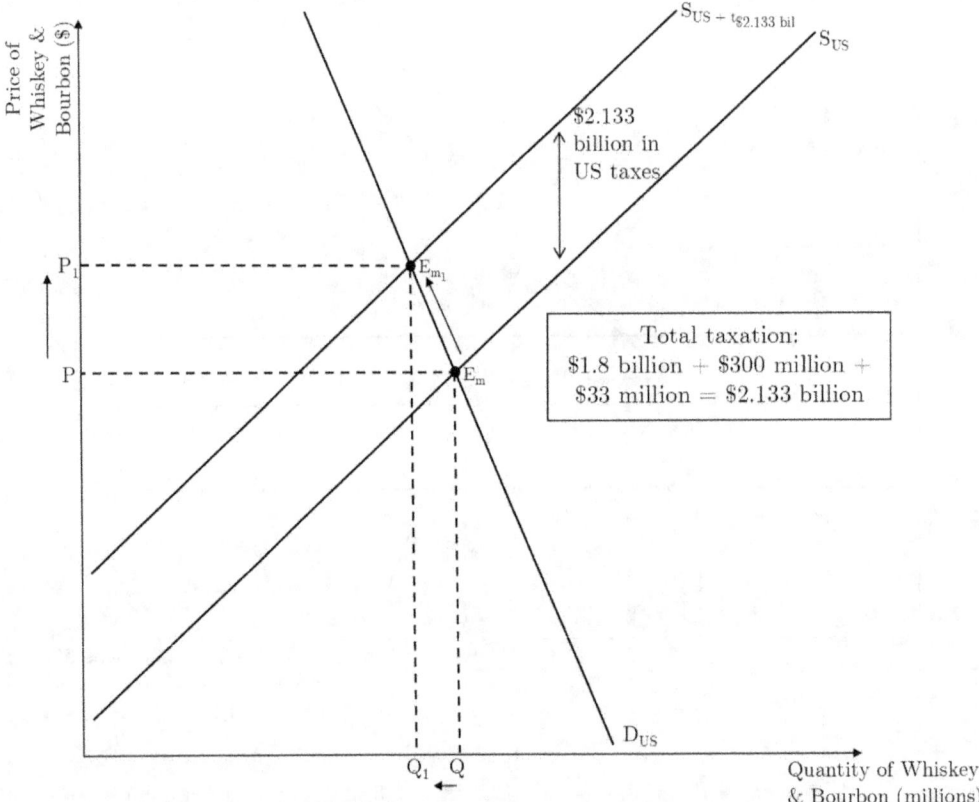

Figure 2: US Whiskey and Bourbon Market with domestic taxes

Domestic taxes, totalling $2.133 billion, cause rising business costs for US distilleries which causes a inward shift of supply from S_{US} to $S_{US + t_{\$2.133\ bil}}$ and forms a new market equilibrium at E_{m_1} which, most notably raises prices, from P to P₁ which places US distillers at a "competitive disadvantage" internationally. Therefore, whilst the existing tariff has already caused substantial damage through the lost export revenue, further increases would be "crippling" to the industry and would "force some distillers out of the European market" as they are no longer able to compete with these higher tariffs. This would mean some unemployment arises from US distillers reducing production but the extent of unemployment depends on the type of whiskey produced as bourbon can only be produced in Kentucky meaning unemployment here is unlikely but for other whiskey producers, which are more vulnerable to foreign competition, unemployment is more likely.

Whilst the imposition of the higher tariffs could be regarded as **equitable** if the EU was protecting their newly emerging domestic whiskey industry, this is highly unlikely considering that bourbon has been targeted due to it being "uniquely American". This means it is more likely that the tariff is imposed purely in a retaliatory sense due to "steel and aluminium disputes". Furthermore, this emphasises another problem with the **equity** of the decision undertaken by the EU since the whiskey industry is suffering "collateral damage" from trade disputes in unrelated industries. However, earlier decisions by the US to also impose tariffs on the EU may mean that the imposition of new tariffs is **equitable** as a leverage mechanism in negotiations, as long as they are only used to try and reduce or remove existing tariffs.

Additionally, the proposed tariff imposition by the EU may raise further issues regarding **equity** as there is a negative impact not only on US distilleries but also on "EU and UK restaurants, bars and consumers" who all suffered from the original tariff and now suffer even more due to the increased tariff since they must now pay a higher price, $P_{US + t_{50\%}}$, instead of the cheaper price, $P_{US + t_{25\%}}$. Furthermore, tariffs act as a regressive tax since the amount paid as a proportion of income falls as incomes rise. This would mean that **equity** in the distribution of income may worsen but since this is only one market it is unlikely to have a very significant impact overall.

Ultimately, the few benefits gained from the tariff through the increased tax revenue for the EU and the slight decrease in the consumption of demerit goods are significantly outweighed by the destructive, **inequitable** effects. The escalation of tariffs is unsustainable and a more **equitable** solution is for discussions to take place to try and resolve trade disputes.

6. PORTFOLIO SIX

Author: Anonymous
Moderated Mark: 41/45
Level: Economics HL

Commentary number	1
Title of the article	Drug Price Regulator Caps Prices of Liquid Medical Oxygen, Medical Oxygen Cylinders
Source of the article	Bloomberg quint https://www.bloombergquint.com/politics/nppa-caps-price-of-liquid-medical-oxygen-medical-oxygen-cylinders
Date article was published	26th September, 2020
Date commentary was written	26th April 2021
Word count (800 Maximum)	798
Section of the syllabus the article relates to	Microeconomics

IA Microeconomics

Title: Drug Price Regulator Caps Prices of Liquid Medical Oxygen, Medical Oxygen Cylinders

Author: The Press Trust of India (PTI)

Date published: 26th September, 2020

Key concepts: Economic well-being

Source: https://www.bloombergquint.com/politics/nppa-caps-price-of-liquid-medical-oxygen-medical-oxygen-cylinders

Article: To ensure availability of medical oxygen in the country at a reasonable price amidst the Covid-19 pandemic, the National Drug Pricing Regulator (NPPA) has capped the price of medical oxygen cylinders and liquid medical oxygen for six months, the government said on Saturday.

The present situation of Covid-19 has resulted in increased demand of medical oxygen by almost four times from 750 MT per day to around 2,800 MT per day, the Ministry of Chemicals and Fertilizers said in a statement.

The issue related to availability, including pricing of oxygen, has been under the continued consideration of Empowered Group 2, Government of India.

It recommended the National Pharmaceutical Pricing Authority (NPPA) to consider capping the ex-factory price of liquid medical oxygen in order to ensure its supply to fillers at reasonable prices, it added.

The Empowered Group 2 also requested NPPA to consider a cap for ex-factory price of oxygen in cylinders in order to ensure supply of oxygen cylinders from fillers at reasonable prices, the Ministry said.

The Ministry of Health & Family Welfare delegated powers under Section 10(2) (l) of Disaster Management Act, 2005 to NPPA to take all necessary steps to immediately regulate the availability and pricing of liquid medical oxygen (LMO) and medical oxygen in cylinders, it added. The regulator deliberated upon the matter in its extraordinary meeting held on September 25 and decided to invoke extraordinary powers in public interest, under Para 19 of DPCO, 13 and under Section 10(20) (l) of Disaster Management Act, 2005 to deal with the emergent situation arising due to the pandemic, the statement said. It decided to immediately regulate the availability and pricing of LMO and medical oxygen cylinders.

NPPA decided "to cap the ex-factory price of LMO at manufacturers end at Rs 15.22/cubic meter (CUM) exclusive of GST, and to further cap the ex-factory cost of medical oxygen cylinder at filler end at Rs. 25.71/CUM exclusive of GST in suppression of the existing ceiling price of Rs. 17.49/CUM, "subject to transportation cost fixation at state level, for six months," the statement said.

The existing rate contracts of state governments for oxygen purchase, as applicable, shall continue, in consumer interest, it added.

The ex-factory price cap of LMO and oxygen gas cylinders will be applicable to domestic production and supply, the statement said.

Date written: 26th April 2021

In India, the Covid-19 pandemic resulted in demand for medical oxygen (MO) to rise to four

times its initial demand of 750 Megatons (MT), drastically raising prices. India's National

Pharmaceutical Pricing Authority (NPPA) imposed a price ceiling, a legal maximum price that

can be charged on a particular product, of Rs.25.71/cubic meter (CUM), replacing an older

ceiling price of Rs.17.49/CUM, on the price of ex-factory MO cylinders, to **ensure economic**

well-being, the level of economic prosperity and standards of living within the country, wherein

economic agents interact with one another to improve their well-being.

Figure 1: Market for medical oxygen (MO) cylinders in India

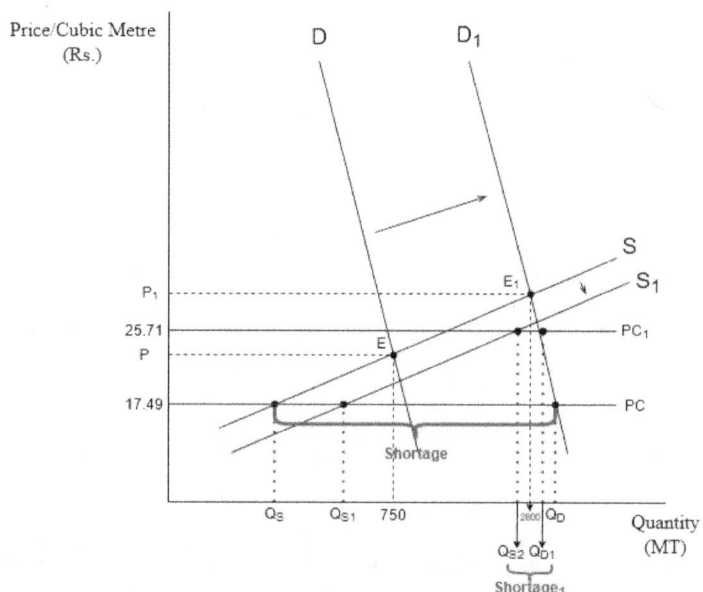

Figure-1 shows the impact of price ceilings on the market for MO cylinders in India. Before the Covid-19 pandemic in India, the market equilibrium was at the intersection of demand curve D, a graphical representation of the willingness and ability of consumers to purchase MO, and supply curve S, a graphical representation of the willingness and ability of producers to supply MO, whereby the price was P and quantity traded was 750MT. Post Covid-19, demand for MO increased drastically, resulting in the demand curve shifting rightward to D_1, creating a new market equilibrium, E_1, whereby price of MO rose to P_1 and the quantity traded rose to 2800MT. Because this price made MO, a necessity, unaffordable for a large majority of consumers, the NPPA of India decided to impose a price ceiling of Rs.17.49/CUM on it to ensure consumer **well-being**. Due to this, producers' profit margins fell, and supply of MO fell to Q_S MT, whereas consumers' demand rose to Q_D MT, as seen in Figure-1. In order to reduce the severity of the shortage that arose due to the ceiling, the government began direct provision of MO to consumers, resulting in the supply curve shifting rightwards to S_1. As a result, supply of MO with the price ceiling in place increased to Q_{S1}. In September 2020 a new ceiling price of Rs.25.71/CUM was introduced. This encouraged producers to increase supply to Q_{S2}, whilst reducing consumers' quantity demanded to Q_{D1}. Theoretically, the current shortage is between Q_{D1} and Q_{S2}.

The introduction of a price ceiling ensures that Covid-19 patients and hospitals receive MO at affordable prices, this encourages **economic well-being** by preventing the healthcare system in India from becoming overwhelmed. However, because the ceiling price exists below the market equilibrium, it distorts the efficient allocation of resources within the market. In this context, it means that there is a shortage of MO, as seen in figure-1. Raising the price ceiling by Rs.8.22 and direct provision of MO by the government greatly reduced this shortage, as represented by the decrease from 'shortage' to 'shortage$_1$' in figure-1. Nevertheless, the gap between supply and demand should be reduced further to ensure consumer **well-being**. This could be done through the import of MO cylinders into India. The article, however, mentions that "The ex-factory price cap of LMO and oxygen gas cylinders will be applicable to domestic production and supply", thus presenting the likelihood of imported oxygen gas being too expensive for consumers, as it will be unaffected by the price ceiling. Alternatively, the government could ensure a smooth supply chain of MO by reallocating the oxygen used for industrial purposes towards medical use when required, although this could adversely affect economic growth.

MO producers in India could also be provided with subsidies and other kinds of financial support like grants, in order to keep costs -and thus prices- low, in lieu of a price ceiling. Subsidies and grants could, however, present an opportunity cost to the government.

The steep demand curve shown in Figure-1 represents the in-elasticity of demand for MO in India, as it's a necessity. Its indispensable nature, therefore, could also cause a rise in black marketeering. Consumers may be forced to purchase MO at higher prices from informal markets due to the shortage, and producers may be more likely to engage in profiteering. To prevent this, hoarding laws aimed at producers and black market regulation may be necessary.

Furthermore, the increase in demand of MO nation-wide makes an increase in logistical costs to producers inevitable, which they may transfer onto consumers. The price ceiling being "subject to transportation cost fixation" ensures that consumers do not have to pay large fees for the transport of MO, which is meant to maintain economic **well-being**. However, the price ceiling is exclusive of other unforeseen expenses such as overheads, and consumers may be forced to pay these additional fees. Producers may also choose to maintain their pre-price ceiling revenues by increasing surcharges, meaning that the ceiling alone will not be enough to regulate prices.

Therefore, the government may need to ensure the regulation of the costs associated with the transport/distribution/production of LMO whilst also making sure that producer **well-being** is not simultaneously affected by providing them with financial support.

Word count: 798

Commentary number	2
Title of the article	Govt recommends anti-dumping duty on some aluminium products from China
Source of the article	Reuters https://www.reuters.com/world/asia-pacific/skorea-cbank-expects-policy-rate-hike-slow-household-debt-growth-2021-09-09
Date article was published	9th September 2021
Date commentary was written	Date written: 26th October 2021
Word count (800 Maximum)	794
Section of the syllabus the article relates to	Macroeconomics

Economics HL

IA Macroeconomics

Title: S.Korea C.bank expects policy rate hike to slow household debt growth

Authors: Cynthia Kim & Ana Nicolaci da Costa

Date published: September 9th, 2021

Key concept: Government intervention

Source: https://www.reuters.com/world/asia-pacific/skorea-cbank-expects-policy-rate-hike-slow-household-debt-growth-2021-09-09

Article:

SEOUL, Sept 9 (Reuters) - South Korea's central bank said on Thursday raising its policy interest rate should help slow the pace of household debt growth going forward, and reiterated that it will continue to tighten policy as inflationary pressures persist.

The Bank of Korea raised its policy rate by 25 basis points to 0.75% in August, hiking for the first time in almost three years to become the first major Asian central bank to shift away from pandemic-era monetary stimulus.

The central bank said in a monetary policy report that a 25 basis point rate hike should help trim household debt growth by 0.4 percentage points within the first 12 months, signalling conditions are building for further policy tightening.

The BOK said it would gradually adjust monetary policy going forward given "inflation is expected (to) accelerate above 2% for the time being."

South Korea's consumer prices rose 2.6% in August from a year earlier, according to recent data, above the central bank's official inflation target of 2%.

Rate cuts worth 75 basis points since last year and ample fiscal stimulus have helped fuel South Korea's strong recovery from the COVID-19 pandemic, putting the BOK at the forefront of stimulus withdrawal globally.

With the economy now on relatively healthy footing, policymakers have flagged in recent weeks the possibility of more rate hikes amid a debt binge in the country. In the June quarter, bank lending to households saw the biggest annual increase since the central bank began releasing relevant data in 2003. Analysts expect the BOK to raise interest rates further this year and next, according to a Reuters poll conducted in late August, with most seeing the base rate at 1.25% by the end of 2022.

<u>Commentary</u>

Date written: 26th October 2021

In South Korea, the government introduced fiscal stimulus, the reduction of taxes and/or an increase in government spending to boost economic activity, coupled with interest rate cuts worth 75 basis-points to help spur a recovery from the Covid-19 pandemic. Soon after, however, household borrowing reached record levels and the inflation rate, the rate of change in price levels over time, reached 2.6% - above the government's target of 2%. In order to return the economy to sustainable levels of output, the Bank of Korea (BOK), the monetary authority of S.Korea, introduced contractionary monetary policy (CMP), a hike in interest rates to reduce economic activity, by raising policy rates, the cost that commercial banks have to incur to borrow money from the central bank, to 0.75% from previous rates of 0.5%, and will further raise them to 1.25% by 2022. This was a form of **government intervention-** government regulations and policies aimed at impacting the outcome of free markets to achieve macroeconomic goals.

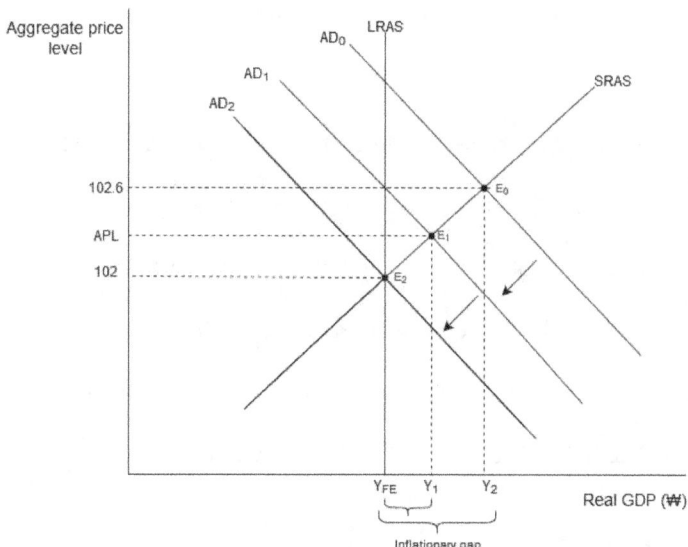

Figure 1: The South Korean Economy

Figure-1 represents the effect of BOK's increase in policy rates on the South Korean economy. During the beginning of the economy's recovery from the Covid-19 pandemic, the equilibrium output (E_0) was at the intersection of the aggregate demand curve (AD_0) which is composed of Consumption(C), Investment(I), Government expenditure(G), Net-exports(X-M), and the Short-term aggregate supply curve (SRAS) at consumer price levels of 2.6% and a real GDP of Y_2₩.

However, the potential of the economy is represented by the perfectly in-elastic LRAS curve, the long-run aggregate supply; the potential output of the economy when all factors of production are optimally used. This difference between the potential output and the actual current output of S.Korea represents the inflationary gap, and the **government intervened** by raising policy rates, in order to bridge this gap. In theory, owing to the **intervention**, as policy rates increase, commercial banks should also raise their interest rates as the rise in policy rates is a direct increase in their costs. Subsequently, borrowing will become more expensive and saving will result in higher returns. As private individuals and firms reduce their spending in favor of saving, both investment (I) and consumption (C) will fall. Additionally, the rise in interest rates could mean that foreigners may seek to invest in S.Korean financial assets, putting upward pressure on the S.Korean ₩. The effect of this is a fall in net-exports (X-M) as imports become cheaper than exports, assuming that the price-elasticity of the exports and imports exceeds one. As these three components of aggregate demand fall, AD_0 will shift leftwards to AD_1, creating a new equilibrium E_1, where the inflation rate should fall to APL and GDP should fall to Y_1₩. However, this shift alone may not be enough for the economy to return to a full level of employment and the government may have to further raise policy rates as mentioned in the article, "most seeing the base rate at 1.25% by the end of 2022." This may lead to a further decrease in aggregate demand from AD_1 to AD_2, whereby aggregate price level and GDP are likely to be 2% and Y_{FE}, the full-employment level of output, owing to the **intervention**.

The use of CMP to lower inflation and "help slow the pace of household debt growth" may be effective given the ease of implementing CMP as compared to contractionary fiscal policy owing to lack of political pressures in the former. The effects of CMP also tend to become visible faster than other forms of **government intervention** as its effects can be anticipated by private individuals and firms beforehand. CMP is also more effective against demand-pull inflation, which was the type of inflation that materialized after the Covid-19 pandemic in the country.

However, the effectiveness of **intervention** is also dependent on the tools used to implement it. The South Korean government's method of increasing policy rates in increments could allow the government to fine-tune the economy without receiving results that are too drastic. However, it's also important to consider whether this incremental increase is too slow for the government to achieve the results it's hoping to receive through **intervention**. It's also possible that the government may not achieve its objectives with this policy due to the near-zero (0.25%) increase in policy rates- which may be too low to bring about significant changes in saving and borrowing, causing household debt levels and inflation rates to remain unaffected.

Furthermore, during phases of economic growth and rising inflation rates, consumer and business confidence tends to be high, meaning that minor hikes in interest rates such as this may be insufficient to curb consumer spending and investment in the economy – limiting the impacts of **government intervention**. This is also why the S.Korean government is considering further hikes in interest rates to reach their objectives.

Word count: **794**

Commentary number	3
Title of the article	Govt recommends anti-dumping duty on some aluminium products from China
Source of the article	Business Today https://www.businesstoday.in/latest/economy/story/govt-recommends-anti-dumping-duty-on-some-aluminium-products-from-china-306401-2021-09-10
Date article was published	10th September 2021
Date commentary was written	Date written: 30th December 2021
Word count (800 Maximum)	797
Section of the syllabus the article relates to	International Economics

Economics HL
IA International Economics

Title: Govt recommends anti-dumping duty on some aluminium products from China

Author: 'Agencies'

Date published: 10th September 2021

Key concept: Choice

Source: https://www.businesstoday.in/latest/economy/story/govt-recommends-anti-dumping-duty-on-some-aluminium-products-from-china-306401-2021-09-10

Article:

The commerce ministry's investigation arm DGTR has recommended the imposition of anti-dumping duty on certain aluminium products from China to guard domestic manufacturers from cheap imports.

The Directorate General of Trade Remedies (DGTR) has concluded in its probe that the dumped imports of 'Certain Flat-Rolled Products of Aluminium' from China have impacted the domestic industry.

The material injury suffered by the domestic industry has been caused by the dumped imports, DGTR has said in a notification.

"The Authority, therefore, considers it necessary to recommend imposition of the definitive anti-dumping duty...on all imports of the subject goods...originating in or exported from China," it added.

The DGTR has recommended USD 65 per tonne and USD 449 per tonne on imports. The finance ministry takes the final decision to impose the duty.

In international trade parlance, dumping happens when a country or a firm exports an item at a price lower than the price of that product in its domestic market. Dumping impacts the price of that product in the importing country, hitting the margins and profits of the manufacturing firms.

According to global trade norms, a country is allowed to impose tariffs on such dumped products to provide a level-playing field to domestic manufacturers. The duty is imposed only after a thorough investigation by a quasi-judicial body, such as DGTR, in India.

The imposition of anti-dumping duty is permissible under the World Trade Organization (WTO) regime. India and China are members of this Geneva-based organisation, which deals with global trade norms.

The duty is aimed at ensuring fair trading practices and creating a level-playing field for domestic producers vis-a-vis foreign producers and exporters.

Commentary

Date written: 30th December 2021

In light of findings that the Indian aluminium industry was suffering "material injury" due to China's dumping practices, a practice where "a country or a firm exports an item at a price lower than the price of that product in its domestic market", the Indian government levied anti-dumping tariffs, a form of direct, protectionist taxes that are imposed by a domestic government to reduce unfair international competition, on Chinese aluminium products; these tariffs were valued at USD 65 and USD 449/tonne, depending on the producer. This action taken by the government is an example of **choice,** the decisions that economic agents have to make due to the scarce nature of resources; these **choices** create opportunity cost.

Figure-1: *The effect of an anti-dumping tariff on the aluminium market in India*

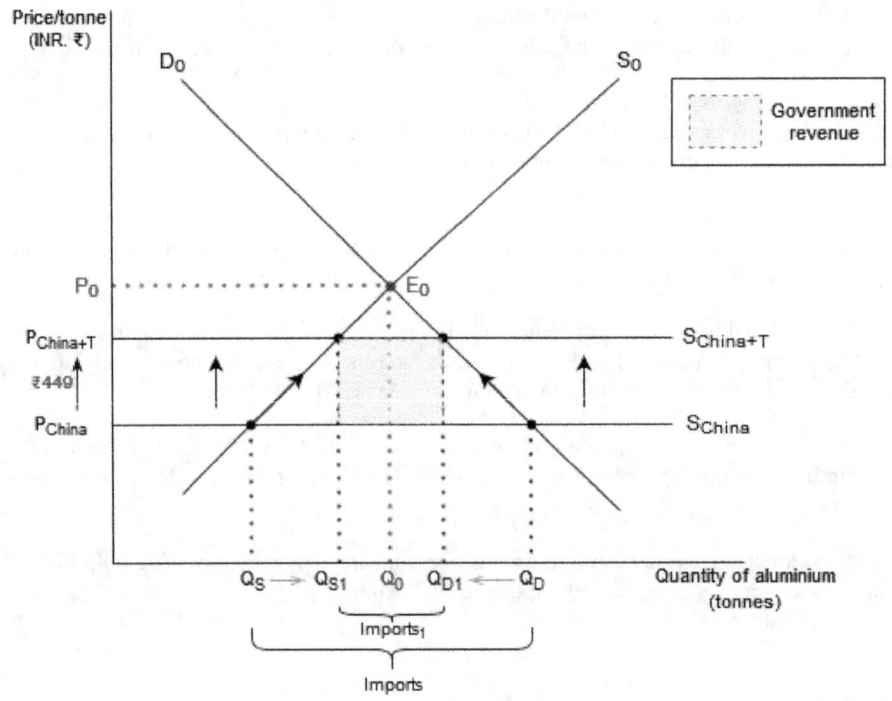

Figure-1 represents the effect of China's dumping practices and the subsequent effect of an anti-dumping tariff on Chinese imports on the market for aluminium in India. The original domestic market equilibrium, E_0, existed at the intersection of the domestic supply curve, S_0, and demand curve D_0, where aluminium was sold at a price of P_0 and quantity of Q_0 tonnes. However, due to China's dumping practices, a new supply curve S_{China} was introduced and thus consumers **preferred** to buy aluminium at the lower price of P_{China}. This disrupted the market equilibrium and caused domestic demand to increase to Q_D, whilst reducing domestic supply to Q_S at China's price level. The shortage caused by the gap in supply and demand had to be met through imports, as seen by the distance Q_D-Q_S. However, imports have significant adverse effects on the economy, including the loss of revenue they cause for domestic aluminium producers. To mitigate this, the Indian government **chose** to levy a tariff on aluminium imports from china of \$449/tonne. As tariffs are considered an increase in the cost of production for foreign suppliers, the supply curve shifted upwards to $S_{China+T}$, which resulted in a price increase of Chinese aluminium from P_{China} to $P_{china+T}$. At this higher price, domestic suppliers were able to increase their supply from Q_S to Q_{S1}, whereas the rise in price led to consumers **choosing** to reduce their demand for aluminium from Q_D to Q_{D1}. This reduced the shortage in the market and the number of imports of aluminium dropped to imports$_1$.

The implementation of a tariff on Chinese imports could be beneficial for domestic producers in India. The tariffs will reduce Chinese competition and allow Indian aluminium manufacturers to continue production at higher price levels. In addition to that, infant industries that would not have been able to sustain themselves in the face of foreign competition will now have the opportunity to attain economies of scale for themselves. Not only will this lead to growth within the domestic aluminium industry but it will also increase employment and prevent structural unemployment within the economy, potentially leading to higher GDP and improved standards of living within the country.

However, as the primary suppliers of aluminium in India become domestic producers, the risk of misallocation of resources increases. It is possible that China has a greater comparative advantage in the production of aluminium and that Indian suppliers cannot produce as efficiently as them. This could lead to higher costs of production due to inefficiency. Additionally, the imposition of a tariff might lead to a fall in foreign competition, which could cause complacency within the domestic aluminium industry and could prevent it from becoming self-sufficient. This could increase inefficiency and reduce export-competitiveness. However, as seen by the blue shaded region in Figure-1, the imposition of a tariff acts as a source of government revenue, which could be used to provide financial assistance to domestic suppliers in order to make them more efficient.

It is also important to consider that this **decision** could lead to retaliatory tariffs by the Chinese government in order to recover the losses caused by the tariffs on their exported aluminium. Not only could this increase the risk of imported inflation, a rise in general price levels due to high costs of key imported commodities, but could also negatively impact India's balance of payments.

Furthermore, it can be difficult, and often expensive, to prove dumping as production costs vary between countries. If the World Trade Organisation (WTO) feels that India's claims of China's dumping practices are unfounded, it could lead to questioning and lengthy dispute settlement hearings. However, since the article mentions that "the duty is imposed only after a thorough investigation", India's **decision** may remain unchallenged.

Ultimately, tariffs may be useful in protecting the domestic industry and generating employment

in the economy. However, the Indian government must guard against misallocation of resources

by providing financial support to firms in India. In the long-run, the tariffs could induce

retaliation and trade-wars but could allow domestic producers to create "a level-playing field" in

the short-term until free-trade continues again.

Word count: 797

7. PORTFOLIO SEVEN

Author: Jason Surakka
Moderated Mark: 41/45
Level: Economics HL

Analysing Boris Johnson's proposed carbon tax

Commentary	1
Title of article	New Carbon taxes: meat, cheese and gas heating prices to rise
Source of article	Source of the article: The Times https://www.thetimes.co.uk/article/new-carbon-tax tes-meat-cheese-and-gas-heating-prices-to-rise-wx z5vd6k2 (Accessed 4 February 2021)
Date the article was published	4 February 2021
Date the commentary was written	8 February 2021
Word count of the commentary	799
Unit of the syllabus to which the article relates	Microeconomics
Key concept being used	Sustainability

New carbon taxes: meat, cheese and gas heating prices to rise

Cheese making could be one of the industries charged for their carbon emissions as the "polluter pays" principle is expanded to all sectors of the economy.

Consumers face higher prices on meat, cheese and gas heating under plans being drawn up by Boris Johnson for new carbon taxes and charges.

The prime minister has ordered every department to produce a "price" for carbon emissions across all areas of the economy as part of a drive to achieve his net-zero carbon pledge. The proposals are at the centre of the carbon reduction blueprint that is expected to be announced in the run-up to Cop26, the United Nations' climate change conference being hosted by Britain in Glasgow in November.

Only heavy industry, power generators and airlines are charged for their carbon emissions at present. However, ministers want to expand the "polluter pays" principle to all sectors, which could lead to higher consumer bills on some of the most carbon-intensive goods and services. This would mean a de facto carbon tax or charge on products such as beef, lamb and cheese.

The proposals could also lead to a switch from climate change levies on electricity bills to taxes on more heavily polluting forms of heating, such as gas. At present environmental and social charges account for 23 per cent of electricity bills, compared with 2 per cent for gas.

A Whitehall memo seen by The Times reveals that Downing Street and the Treasury have asked all departments for plans for a carbon-pricing scheme across all areas of the economy.

"The chancellor and the prime minister want a sector-by-sector view on how we could implement some form of carbon pricing and an overall road map to deliver [it] in the next decade," the memo states. It suggests that these could include a direct "carbon tax".

The proposals put forward by government departments will form part of an overall strategy to "deliver a carbon price for the whole economy" that is due to be announced by the prime minister before the UN climate conference.

One source close to the government's thinking said that Britain's plans could be used to persuade other countries to follow suit as part of the international move towards net zero.

"The big driver for this is that if you can get a decent chunk of countries to agree to some kind of carbon price floor then you can finally have an [international] system that encompasses all the big competitive industries and potentially agriculture," the source said.

One of the concerns in developed countries such as Britain is that imposing carbon taxes on industries could put them at a competitive disadvantage against nations that do not have the same financial penalties.

The EU has already raised the prospect of introducing a carbon border adjustment that would levy charges on products from countries that do not impose penalties for emissions.

Britain is investigating such measures but would prefer an international approach that could be delivered through Cop26. Although Britain's plan has yet to be formalised the government wants to use its chairmanship of the conference to push the issue up the international agenda.

Experts welcomed the move but warned yesterday that ministers would need to ensure that the burden of new domestic taxes and charges did not hit those least able to pay.

Katie White, executive director of the World Wildlife Fund, said the government needed to ensure that families were supported: "Carbon taxes could be a bold and effective way to accelerate the low-carbon transition, but the government must ensure families don't lose out and businesses are supported to make the move to a clean and prosperous economy."

Darren Jones, chairman of the Commons business select committee, said he supported the concept of carbon pricing as it was an "important part of achieving net zero". But he added: "What we wouldn't want to do is undermine that by acting too quickly with carbon pricing that could see a very significant change in consumer costs."

Jess Ralston, an analyst at the energy and climate intelligence unit, said that the government's move was significant, adding: "If we are going to meet net zero we need to see all parts of the economy decarbonising and a blanket carbon tax would help with that."

Analysis
Downing Street knows profound changes must be made now if the UK is to meet its pledge to achieve net-zero emissions by 2050. Central to this is a plan to put a carbon "price" — an effective pollution tax — on all aspects of the UK economy.

This is likely to have long-term ramifications for two key areas: domestic gas heating and food. Polluting gas could shoulder more of the "green tax" burden, perhaps through a straight carbon tax on bills, while a rise in food prices to reflect the high carbon cost of agriculture — which generated 10 per cent of UK greenhouse gas emissions in 2017 — would force farmers and consumers to think differently.

Commentary:

This commentary, through the lens of '**sustainability**', analyses Boris Johnson's proposed carbon-tax targeted towards all sectors of the economy. It focuses on carbon-taxes, taxes per unit of carbon-emissions of fossil fuels to deal with the problems of climate change and promote **sustainable** use of common-pool resources (Tragakes, 5.3), and how that will affect future producers' ability to produce goods and services by using alternative resources. Carbon-emissions are negative-externalities of consumption and production, since both consumers and producers use them, causing negative environmental effects on third-parties. This commentary concludes that carbon-taxes **sustainably** decarbonise the economy by incentivising alternative resources, whilst increasing prices for consumers and costs for producers.

Boris Johnson's proposed carbon-tax is "to achieve net-zero carbon pledge". In Figure 1, production and consumption of carbon-products currently reduces Britain's production possibilities from PPC1 to PPC2 (i.e. cheese and gas heating), because **unsustainable** consumption patterns decrease Britain's production possibilities; in the long-run, this **unsustainably** reduces natural capital by decreasing quantity and quality of resources, adding the need for a carbon-tax.

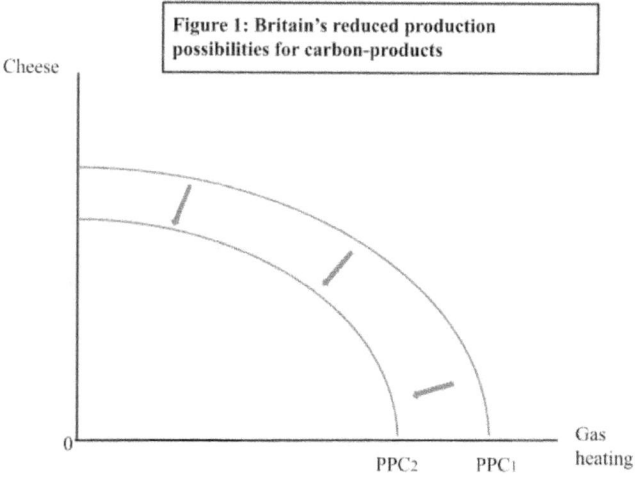

Cheese

Figure 1: Britain's reduced production possibilities for carbon-products

0

PPC2   PPC1

Gas heating

175

In Figure 2, marginal private benefits (MPB) exceed marginal social benefits (MSB), because firms produce above social optimum. The supply curve is relatively inelastic because of the time it takes to produce carbon-products, and the demand curves are relatively inelastic because carbon-products are deemed as a necessity. Market-failure occurs, as MPB exceeds MSB because both price (Pm) and quantity (Qm) are higher than Popt and Qopt, implying that third-parties face negative-externalities. Carbon-emitting products, like heaters, are often a necessity and now have an increased equilibrium-price, because of increased costs of production that increase prices and, ideally, incentivise consumers to use **sustainable** alternatives (like renewable energy) that the government can subsidise with the revenue it collects (area a+b+c+d+e+f).

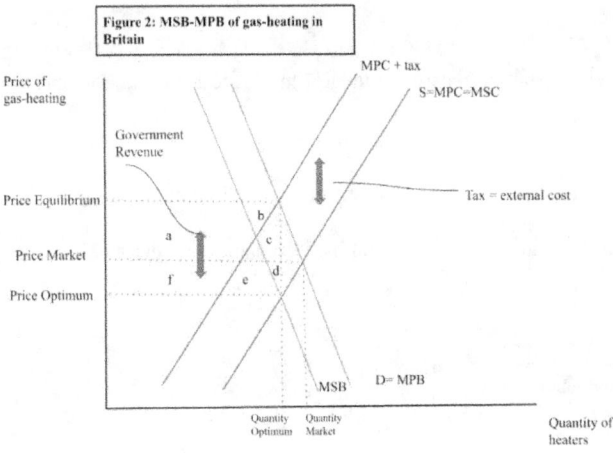

In Figure 3, the carbon-tax shifts supply-curve inwards, increasing costs of production and thus price of goods, incentivising producers to shift to alternatives or producing less, hence leading to **sustainable** outcomes. Taxes increase costs of production, decreasing quantity produced, increasing prices, and shifting supply from MPC to MSC1. However, if carbon-dependent firms (e.g. heating-firms) switch to alternatives- more **sustainable** resources- Qopt1 will increase to Qopt2, as external costs of producing the output will diminish. Hence, MSC1 shifts rightward to MSC2, increasing quantity supplied and decreasing price to P2. If the carbon-tax succeeds to shift MSC1 to MSC2, it will create **sustainable** outcomes by promoting alternatives, instead of only increasing prices for consumers.

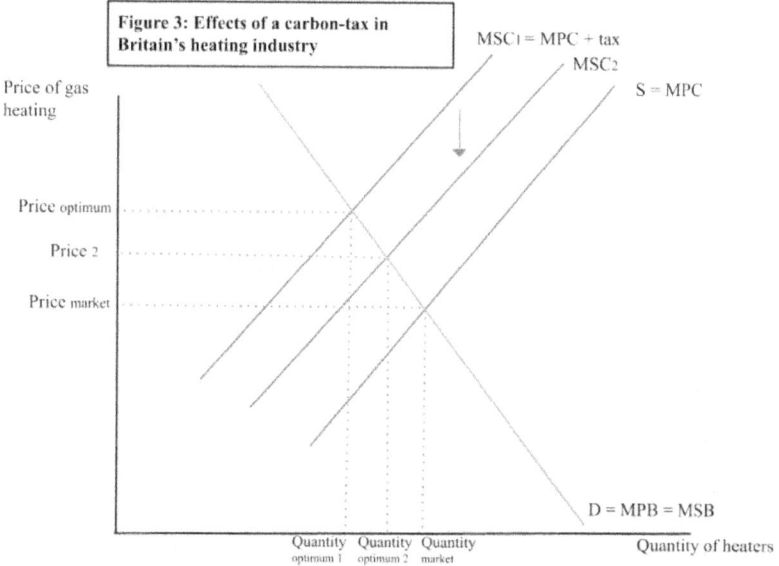

However, a carbon-tax causes few problems to the economy. It increases costs of production and prices for consumers, discourages companies from producing, reduces competitiveness within the market, and might "hit those least able to pay" due to indirect taxes' regressive nature, meaning lower income-groups are taxed at higher proportions than higher income-groups; this economic burden would affect consumers with low incomes more than producers with often high revenues. It might not incentivise other countries to propose a carbon-tax, putting British firms at a "competitive disadvantage", as their costs of production would increase in the global economy. Industries dependent on carbon will also contract; employees might face unemployment, meaning the carbon-tax might be harmful in the long-run, unless firms can cover their costs and find alternative resources against global-warming. However, if both supply and demand cannot reach optimum-levels, it will be inefficient and **unsustainable** when tackling the problems of the environment. Because production costs increase, small firms may face bankruptcy, whilst larger ones may increase their market-power or relocate to countries with lower production costs.

However, carbon-taxes promote the preservation of the environment and result in more **sustainable** outcomes, as land resources are carefully used. Implementing it might be helpful in the long-run if it reduces the possibility of paying for more environment-related destruction in the future; since supply is relatively inelastic, increased costs of production will make firms less responsive to changes in prices in the long-run when all factors of production are variable. Decarbonising the economy also supports **sustainable** alternatives, as those will not be affected by carbon-taxes, and the increase in demand for those goods and services- especially with the help of the indirect tax's government revenue- will then lower prices for consumers. Carbon is a finite and environmentally harmful resource, therefore promoting infinite, **sustainable** resources will, eventually, lower the costs of production; possibly encouraging other countries to follow a similar **sustainable** path.

To conclude, the concept of '**sustainability**' is crucial. For the carbon-tax to work, it must ensure other countries follow along, and that it doesn't hurt British firms in the long-run nor increase prices for consumers too rapidly in the short-run when fewer **sustainable** alternatives are available. To reach "zet-nero", the carbon-tax must be equally effective for consumers and producers to incentivise both to use **sustainable** alternatives so future generations may produce and satisfy their needs and wants in the future.

Commentary	2
Title of article	Bank of England's Saunders: inflation could force interest rate rise next year
Source of article	https://www.theguardian.com/business/2021/sep/07/bank-of-england-saunders-inflation-interest-rate-rise
Date the article was published	September 9, 2021
Date the commentary was written	December 10, 2021
Word count of the commentary	800
Unit of the syllabus to which the article relates	Macroeconomics
Key concept being used	Intervention

Article:

The Bank of England could be forced into action to raise interest rates next year if inflation remains persistently higher than expected, one of Threadneedle Street's policymakers has said.

Michael Saunders, one of nine members of the Bank's monetary policy committee, said a rise in borrowing costs could be warranted before the end of 2022 if the UK's economic recovery from lockdown is maintained and the rate of inflation sticks at elevated levels.

"If the economy continues to recover, and inflation shows signs of being more persistent, then it might be right to think of interest rates going up in the next year or so. But that is not a promise and depends on economic conditions," he told an online event hosted by accountancy software company Intuit.

Signalling concern over a burst of inflationary pressure rippling through the British economy, he said the time was moving closer to withdraw high levels of emergency economic stimulus. However, any rate increase would be "relatively limited".

He added that a rise in borrowing costs next year was "not a promise", as it would need to depend on economic conditions.

Saunders, who voted last month to cut short the Bank's £895bn quantitative easing bond-buying programme, said he was worried that continuing with asset purchases could stoke expectations among households and businesses for inflation to drift higher.

"Such an outcome could well require a more substantial tightening of monetary policy later, and might limit the committee's scope to respond promptly the next time the economy needs more stimulus," he said.

His comments come after Catherine Mann, the newest external rate-setter at the central bank, said inflation would prove less sticky than in the 1970s. Speaking earlier this week, Mann said firms could be more reluctant than in the past to hit households with higher prices for goods and services, and that a historic link between inflation and wages had diminished in recent times.

Financial market expectations were already for a rate rise in 2022 before Saunders's comments, with most City economists anticipating the central bank will move to tame inflationary pressures next year.

Threadneedle Street forecasts inflation could rise close to 4% this year, the highest rate for a decade.

However, much of the increase is down to the economy recovering from its historic slump in 2020, rather than a sharp jump in consumer prices. The Bank expects pressures linked to pandemic disruption to fade over time, bringing inflation back towards its 2% target rate.

Commentary (800):

Through the lens of **'intervention'**, this commentary analyses Bank of England's opportunity to use monetary-policy to reduce inflation, a sustained increase in the general price-level (Tragakes, 5.3), by reducing quantitative-easing. The commentary concludes that while monetary-policy reduces borrowing and spending by firms and consumers in the short-run, the **intervention** will likely increase their confidence and encourage stable economic growth and investment in the long-run.

After the "UK's economic recovery from lockdown", firms and consumers were more willing and able to borrow and spend, increasing aggregate-demand more rapidly than productive capacity, creating bottlenecks thus increasing the price-level (Figure 2). Since high inflation diminishes purchasing-power and consumer and business confidence in the long-run, contractionary monetary-policy may be used in the UK. In Figure 1, the effect of increasing interest-rates can be seen: Bank of England has "cut short the Bank's £895bn quantitative-easing bond-buying programme", reducing bond-purchases, meaning the **intervention** decreases the money-supply and increases interest-rates from i_1 to i_2.

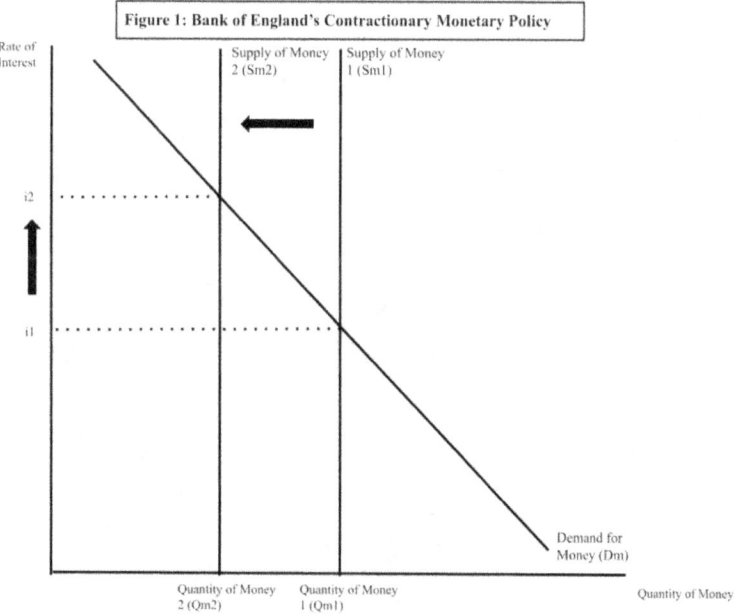

Figure 1: Bank of England's Contractionary Monetary Policy

In Figure 2, the effect of increased interest-rates can be seen on aggregate-demand (AD). Unemployment rate is lower than naturally, at Y_{infl} instead of Y_p, as consumers and firms are maximising the spare capacity within the economy as the borrowing-costs are relatively low, with the average price-level (APL) at APL_1. Since the risk of inflation being "more persistent", an **intervention** in the money-market could reduce APL_1 to APL_2, as interest-rates affect investment, consumer expenditure and net exports. The three components, ceteris paribus, would shift AD1, as the cost of credit would affect the marginal propensity to consume, increased borrowing-costs would make firms less willing and able to invest, and an appreciation of the pound sterling could increase imports and make exports less competitive (i.e. decreasing net exports). The **intervention** would relatively shortly reduce AD_1 to AD_2, reducing national income from Y_{infl} to Y_p and the price-level from APL_1 to APL_2, possibly meeting the "2% target rate", which could reduce investor uncertainty.

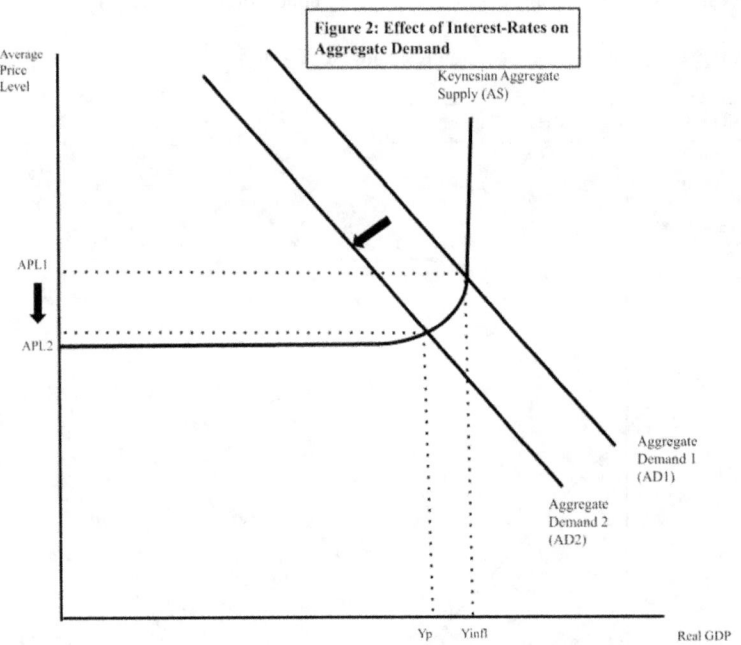

Figure 2: Effect of Interest-Rates on Aggregate Demand

Worrying that inflation will rise to 4%, "the highest rate for a decade", contractionary monetary-policy could potentially reduce AD to meet Bank of England's "2% target rate", impacting firms and consumers in the short-run as borrowing-costs increase. However, in the-long run, this would likely benefit business and consumer confidence as a lower rate of inflation creates a stable environment for saving and investment, promoting long-term economic growth by reducing business cycle fluctuations as more accurate forecasts of the price-level may encourage firms to invest more wisely. In the short-run, it will likely not achieve this, and it's uncertain whether the relatively short time-lags will shift AD_1 precisely to AD_2. If inflation would "prove less sticky than in the 1970s", prices may respond to contractionary monetary-policy more rapidly than expected, allowing AD to shift more rapidly.

However, **intervening** in the money-market might not always be effective. The effectiveness can be hard to measure, especially at times of "economic recovery", where bottlenecks emerge as demand-pull inflation occurs. Moreover, because of the pandemic, AD is increasing because of consumers and firms being more willing and able to spend and invest, increasing the APL; contractionary monetary-policy reduces business confidence at a time of recovery, and may have long-run effects- like an increase in unemployment- that are worse than the short-run inflationary concerns. **Intervention** may, therefore, conflict with government objectives, as it will reduce employment and potential output, although a "link between inflation and wages has diminished". Moreover, as a demand-side policy, it doesn't address the supply-side shortages of the pandemic.

Nonetheless, **intervention** in monetary-policy could be advantageous. Since Bank of England is independent, monetary-policy is both incremental and reversible during inflationary pressure, which is helpful if inflation starts to "fade over time". While monetary-policy is prone to time-lags, these are relatively short. Moreover, affecting interest-rates doesn't directly affect budget deficits, which is helpful when recovering from a "historic" recession. However, an increase in the unemployment rate will likely require the government to increase transfer payments, indirectly having a negative effect on the government's budget. However, it would allow the target-rate to be reached, meaning that such an **intervention** could meet government objectives.

To conclude, the concept of **'intervention'** is crucial. Reducing quantitative-easing will reduce the money-supply and increase interest-rates, but its impact on aggregate-demand may be prone to relatively short time-lags at a time of economic expansion; it may also be inefficient, if other monetary tools are still used. Nonetheless, Bank of England's **intervention** in cutting quantitative easing can be efficient to reduce inflation relatively fast and meet their 2% inflation target-rate, while not directly impacting the government budget, though it could indirectly impact it if unemployment increases while potential output decreases. Although it reduces consumer and business borrowing and spending in the short-run, the **intervention** enables a steady 2% inflation-rate in the long-run, promoting a stable environment for long-term economic growth and investment.

Bibliography

"Bank of England's Saunders: Inflation Could Force Interest Rate Rise next Year." The Guardian, 7 Sept. 2021, www.theguardian.com/business/2021/sep/07/bank-of-england-saunders-inflation-interest-rate-rise. Accessed 9 Sept. 2021.

Tragakes, Ellie. *Economics for the IB Diploma*. 30 June 2020. Accessed 11 Sept. 2021

Commentary	3
Title of article	Turkish lira faces a rocky new year as inflation hits 19-year high and could go higher
Source of article	https://www.cnbc.com/2022/01/05/turkish-lira-falls-as-inflation-hits-nearly-two-decade-high.html
Date the article was published	January 5, 2022
Date the commentary was written	March 2, 2022
Word count of the commentary	800
Unit of the syllabus to which the article relates	Global Economy
Key concept being used	Choice

Article

Turkey's lira tumbled again overnight over rising inflation fears, with markets showing little faith in President Recep Tayyip Erdogan's promises that the worst of the country's economic turmoil is over. Inflation in the country of 84 million hit a 19-year high of 36.1% for December, the highest in all of Erdogan's tenure as president. And economists warn it could still go up, thanks to Erdogan's unorthodox policy of cutting and refusing to raise interest rates, a standard tool used by monetary policymakers to cool down rising costs and strengthen local currencies.

The lira was trading at 13.36 to the dollar on Wednesday morning at 11 a.m. in Istanbul, already facing a rocky start to the new year after having lost about 45% of its value against the greenback since the start of 2021, which was its worst year in two decades.

Erdogan last month revealed a new rescue plan to bolster the currency without raising rates, which essentially entails protecting local depositors against market volatility by paying them the difference if the lira's decline against hard currencies surpass banks' interest rates. Critics say this plan is unsustainable, will further deplete Turkey's already low FX reserves, and is essentially one large hidden interest rate hike.

"We've seen time and time again, particularly in emerging markets — foreign investors sell the currency, local investors sell the currency when they think interest rate policy has gone a bit wacky," Christopher Payne, chief economist at Dubai-based Peninsula Real Estate Management, told CNBC on Tuesday. "The result of a collapsing currency is inflation. And there's really no way to escape that."

Food and beverage prices in Turkey are up 44% year-on-year, and consumer prices rose 13.58% in December alone, according to the Turkish Statistical Institute. Some economists predict inflation hitting as high as 50% by the end of the first quarter of 2022 if Turkey's monetary policy — seen as direly lacking independence and controlled by Erdogan — is not reversed. Goldman Sachs sees it going above 40% for most of the coming year.

Erdogan, meanwhile, said he was "saddened" by the dramatic spike in inflation.

But the president continues to brush aside concerns, saying on Tuesday from Ankara that the "excessive" price increases are "thorns" and "pebbles" on Turkey's path, and that his government will get rid of the inflation "bubble." Erdogan added that he is determined to put Turkey in the world's top 10 economies. The country's currency fared the worst out of all emerging market currencies in 2021.

"Closing yourself off to the outside world, and imposing capital controls, is not something Turkey is going to do as an exporting economy," Payne said, referencing measures that some emerging economies have imposed in similar situations.

"There's no getting away from the fact of economics on this one," he said. "Whether President Erdogan will change his mind — or how he will change his mind and prove that he was right all along — is the interesting thing we'll be watching."

187

Commentary

Through the lens of **'choice'**, this commentary analyses lira's depreciation- a decrease in the value of a currency in the context of a floating exchange system- on Turkey's economy. The commentary concludes the **choice** of decreasing interest-rates- depreciating lira- will increase average price-level as net-exports and Turkish firms' costs of production increase and will negatively impact equity, though increasing interest-rates could benefit Turkish firms selling relatively elastic goods domestically and exporters selling relatively inelastic goods.

As President Erdogan has cut and "refus[ed] to raise interest rates," investors will likely sell their lira to countries with higher relative interest-rates to ensure higher rate of returns, increasing financial capital flow, shifting supply of lira from S1 to S2 (Figure 1). Demand for lira will likely decrease from D1 to D2 (Figure 1), as saving deposits in banks and bonds become less attractive to "foreign" and "local investors", reducing financial capital flows. Thus, lira depreciates from ER1 to ER2 (Figure 1), hence "los[s] about 45% of [lira's] value against the [dollar]". Such would make exports relatively cheaper and more appealing to foreign countries, and imports relatively more expensive and less appealing to Turkish consumers and producers; ceteris paribus, net-exports increase, increasing aggregate demand (AD) and average price-level (APL). This would lead to short-run economic growth and increase in national income, as the economy operates beyond natural rate of unemployment, Y2 (figure 2).

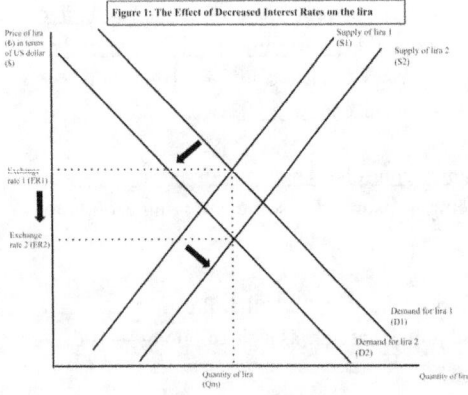

188

However, lira's depreciation has long-run consequences. As imports become relatively more expensive, Turkish producers relying on foreign resources will likely face increases in production costs, as imports become more expensive; if Turkish producers are relatively dependent on imports, this may decrease short-run aggregate supply, also increasing APL from APL1 to APL2 and decreasing real GDP from Y2 to Y1 (Figure 2). **Choice** of cutting interest-rates can be harmful in long-run, as stagflation may occur if both demand-pull and cost-push inflation occur because of lira's depreciation. In long-run, consumer and business confidence could decrease if **choice** of not increasing interest-rates persists, as fewer investors would be willing to invest in Turkey. Such could reduce export revenue as foreigners have "little faith" in Turkey.

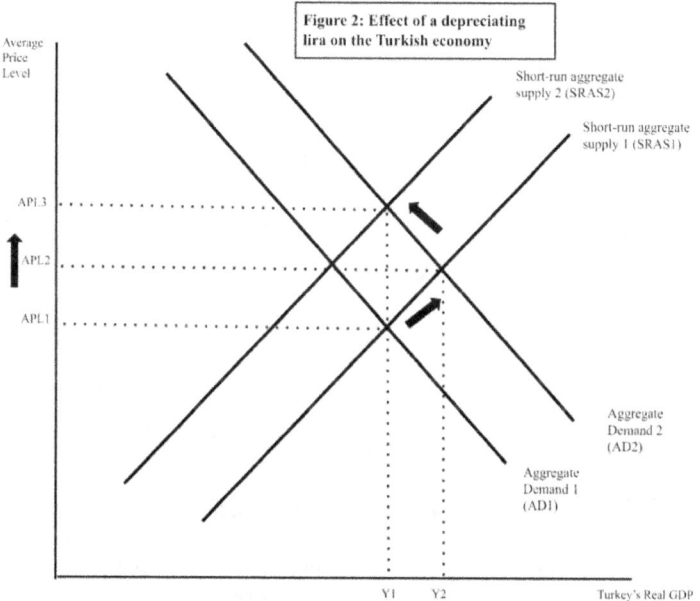

Figure 2: Effect of a depreciating lira on the Turkish economy

Nonetheless, some producers might benefit from **choice** of depreciating lira. If Turkish exporters sell relatively elastic goods, they may face increases in total revenue, as fall in price of good will lead to relatively higher increase in quantity demanded; similarly, Turkish firms selling relatively inelastic goods in Turkey may benefit from increase in average price-level, as increase in price leads to relatively smaller decrease in quantity demanded. Erdogan's **choice** may increase employment in export-industry, as

189

quantity demanded for those goods increases due to lira's depreciation, though increases in

unemployment in domestic industries should be expected. Nonetheless, it's unlikely Turkish firms will

stop importing resources from abroad if they have contracts between foreign firms, potentially limiting

short-run decreases in import expenditure.

If Erdogan's **choice** of cutting interest rates persists, it seems unlikely he can "get rid of the inflation

bubble", as consumption, investment and net-exports would likely increase. In the long-run, fewer firms

would be willing and able to make accurate economic forecasts, impacting consumer and business

confidence, likely reducing their investment and thus long-run economic growth. This is worrisome when

some predictions regarding inflation are "as high as 50% by the end of the first quarter". Furthermore,

choice of depreciation to "put Turkey in the world's top 10 economies" as an "exporting economy" seems

unlikely to happen. Depreciation would increase the value of foreign debt, which increases debt burden on

Turkish individuals. Moreover, rise in inflation, as "consumer prices rose 13.58%", will likely negatively

affect "local investors" as their purchasing power decreases. Turkish firms and income-groups relying on

goods imported from overseas would face increased costs; **choice** of letting lira depreciate might be

inequitable. Hence, for low- and middle-income groups, Erdogan's **choice** may be most impactful, as they

will carry a relatively larger burden.

However, if Erdogan chooses to "get rid of the inflation bubble", the **choice** of increasing interest rates

would be required. Though such would likely appreciate lira and reduce net exports, negatively affecting

the "exporting economy", it would likely lower the rate of inflation and costs of living and production.

To conclude, the concept of **'choice'** is necessary. To not let lira depreciate further, Erdogan's **choice** of

cutting interest rates is important. If interest rates are cut, or not increased, the lira will likely depreciate

and the Turkish economy might face severe consequences; both demand-pull and cost-push inflation

could occur, resulting in stagflation. Turkish producers reliant on foreign resources would face increased costs of production, though some exporters could gain greater total revenues if they sell relatively elastic goods. Consumers would face higher costs of living, and both business and consumer confidence would be lowered in the long-run, though such could be rectified by potential interest-rate rise.

Bibliography

Turak, Natasha. "Turkish Lira Faces a Rocky New Year as Inflation Hits 19-Year High and Could Go Higher." CNBC, 5 Jan. 2022, www.cnbc.com/2022/01/05/turkish-lira-falls-as-inflation-hits-nearly-two-decade-high.html. Accessed 6 Jan. 2022

Tragakes, Ellie. *Economics for the IB Diploma*. 30 June 2020. Accessed 18 Jan. 2022

www.ingramcontent.com/pod-product-compliance
Lightning Source LLC
Chambersburg PA
CBHW080849120626
46546CB00008B/2758

* 9 7 8 1 9 9 9 6 1 1 5 7 6 *